COUNTRIES OF THE WORLD

India

Gareth Stevens Publishing
MILWAUKEE

8745499

About the Author: Sunandini Arora Lal, a native of New Delhi, India, is a professional freelance writer and editor. She has a diploma in writing for children and teenagers from the Institute of Children's Literature in West Redding, Connecticut.

Written by
SUNANDINI ARORA LAL

Edited by
LEELA VENGADASALAM

Designed by
LYNN CHIN NYUK L!NG

Picture research by
SUSAN JANE MANUEL

First published in North America in 1999 by
Gareth Stevens Publishing
1555 North RiverCenter Drive, Suite 201
Milwaukee, Wisconsin 53212 USA

For a free color catalog describing
Gareth Stevens' list of high-quality books
and multimedia programs, call
1-800-542-2595 (USA) or
1-800-461-9120 (CANADA).
Gareth Stevens Publishing's
Fax: (414) 225-0377.
See our catalog, too, on the World Wide Web:
gsinc.com

© **TIMES EDITIONS PTE LTD 1999**
Originated and designed by
Times Books International
an imprint of Times Editions Pte Ltd
Times Centre, 1 New Industrial Road
Singapore 536196
http://www.timesone.com.sg/te

Library of Congress Cataloging-in-Publication Data
Arora Lal, Sunandini,
India / by Sunandini Arora Lal.
p. cm. -- (Countries of the world)
Includes bibliographical references and index.
Summary: An introduction to the geography, history, economy, culture, and people of the second most populous country in the world, India.
ISBN 0-8368-2262-5 (lib. bdg.)
1. India -- Juvenile literature. [1. India.] I.Title.
II. Series: Countries of the world (Milwaukee, Wis.)
DS407.A76   1999
977.2--dc21   98-35285

Printed in Singapore

1 2 3 4 5 6 7 8 9 03 02 01 00 99

PICTURE CREDITS
Bes Stock: 21, 58
Susanna Burton: 26
Joginder Chawla: 7, 10, 14 (both), 15 (top), 16, 20, 22, 23 (top), 25, 29, 34, 40, 41, 47 (top), 49, 57 (top), 59 (top), 60, 69, 72, 73, 76, 78, 79, 83, 85, 89
Fotomedia: cover, 3 (bottom), 6, 9 (top), 17, 27, 33 (both), 37, 39, 45, 48, 53, 55, 61, 62, 67, 75, 84
The Hutchison Library: 9 (bottom), 28, 42, 57 (bottom), 71
Illustrated London News Picture Library: 12, 15 (bottom), 52
Bjorn Kingwall: 1, 23, 43, 46, 74, 82
Jason Lauré: 63
Christine Osborne Pictures: 2, 3 (center), 5, 8, 11, 64, 65 (both), 70 (both)
Thakur Dalip Singh: 68
Still Pictures: 77, 81
Sylvia Cordaiy Photo Library: 18 (bottom), 19, 30, 35, 44
Liba Taylor Photography: 24, 31
Travel Ink: 47
Trip Photographic Library: 3 (top), 13, 18 (top), 32, 36, 38, 50, 51, 54, 56, 66, 80, 87, 91

Digital Scanning by Superskill Graphics Pte Ltd

Contents

AN OVERVIEW OF INDIA

India is the largest democracy in the world and the second most populous country in the world after China. In its early history, travelers and invaders came to its shores to share in its wealth and rich culture. Some pillaged the land and left, while others, such as the Mughals, stayed. They and the Greeks, Arabs, Afghans, Turks, and Mongols made significant contributions to the country. After gaining independence in 1947 from the British, the Indian government restricted external trade and investments to attain economic self-sufficiency and a balanced distribution of income. The strategy did not work well, so the restrictions were lifted in 1991. Today, India is looking to Asia and the West for trade and investment opportunities.

Opposite: **The Gateway of India near Bombay Harbor. Bombay, now called Mumbai, is the country's financial and commercial center and the main port on the Arabian Sea.**

Below: **Beating the heat and the crowds on Indian roads — this family of four rides on a scooter.**

THE FLAG OF INDIA

The Indian flag is derived from the flag of the Indian National Congress, the party of Mahatma Gandhi and Jawaharlal Nehru; therefore, it is similar to the party flag. The Congress flag was first used in 1933 with the colors saffron for courage and sacrifice, white for truth and peace, and green for faith, fertility, and chivalry. In the center of the white band was the emblem of a wheel spinning. When India gained independence, a Buddhist *dharma chakra* (DHAR-mah CHAK-rah), or wheel of life, replaced the spinning wheel. The dharma chakra, discovered at Sarnath, Uttar Pradesh, dates from the time of Emperor Ashoka (269–232 B.C.).

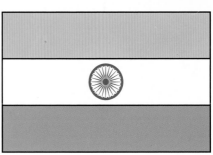

Geography

The Land

India is a peninsula bounded by the Arabian Sea to the west, the Bay of Bengal to the east, and the Indian Ocean to the south. The country is bordered by China, Bhutan, and Nepal to the north. The Himalayas, one of the largest mountain ranges in the world, are also found in the north. On the northwest, India is bordered by Pakistan, and on the east, it is bordered by Bangladesh.

The country is divided into seven major geographical regions. They are the Indo-Gangetic plain, formed by the basins of the Indus, Ganges, and Brahmaputra rivers; the central highlands; the Deccan Plateau in central India, which includes the geologically oldest parts of the country; the Eastern Ghats; the Western Ghats; the Lakshadweep Islands (formerly called the Laccadives) as well as the Andaman and Nicobar islands; and the northern and northeastern mountain ranges, which include the Himalayas.

The states of Jammu and Kashmir, Himachal Pradesh, Uttar Pradesh, Assam, and West Bengal have picturesque Himalayan

Below: **The Himalayas — from the Sanskrit word** *hima*, **meaning "snow," and** *alaya*, **meaning "abode" — extend 1,500 miles (2,414 kilometers) from Kashmir in the west to Assam in the east. They have some of the highest peaks in the world, including Mount Everest in Nepal at 29,028 feet (8,848 meters) and Kanchenjunga on the border between Nepal and Sikkim at 28,208 feet (8,598 m).**

Above: **People bathing in the Ganges River.**

landscapes of snowcapped mountains, waterfalls, wide valleys, and deep river gorges. Although India is often seen as a hot and humid country, it has the world's largest land area of snow and glaciers outside the subpolar regions. The Himalayas have some of the biggest mountain glaciers in the world.

Several rivers run through India. These can be grouped into the Deccan rivers, the Himalayan rivers, the coastal rivers, and the rivers of the inland drainage basin. For Hindus, the Ganges River, also known as the Ganga, is the most sacred of rivers. It originates in the Gangotri glacier in the Himalayas and flows to the heartland of India, the Indo-Gangetic Plain. Because of the plentiful water supply, the plain has rich alluvial soil. It is the most densely populated region in India. In contrast, the triangular region south of the plain is a rocky plateau.

The Deccan rivers fluctuate in volume. Many of them shrink to streams during the hot season. The coastal rivers are short, as are the few rivers of western Rajasthan, which either end in salt lakes or are lost in the sands of the Thar Desert. The Himalayan rivers are snow- and rain-fed, and flow continuously.

Above: **A camel safari travels through the Thar Desert.**

Seasons

From the Himalayas in the north to Kanya Kumari in the south, and from Assam in the east to the salt marshes of the Rann of Kachchh in the west, the climate of India is as varied as its terrain. There are three main seasons: summer from March to May, the rainy season from June to September, and winter from October to February.

Rainfall varies widely in different parts of the country. The foot of the Western Ghats and the states of Arunachal Pradesh, Assam, Manipur, Meghalaya, Mizoram, Nagaland, and Tripura in the northeast experience heavy rainfall and thus have lush vegetation. Cherrapunji in Meghalaya has averaged 450 inches (11,430 millimeters) of rain annually over a 74-year period, which is the highest rainfall recorded in Asia and the second highest in the world! In contrast, the Thar Desert in Rajasthan has an average annual rainfall of only 4 inches (102 mm).

Temperatures also vary widely from one region to another. Himalayan towns, such as Darjeeling and Shimla, have average annual temperatures of 54° Fahrenheit (12° Centigrade), while Palayankottai in the south records an average annual temperature of 85° F (29.5° C).

EMBRACING TREES

Vast forests destroyed. Massive flooding. Food shortages. These are some of the problems faced by rural people in the hills. Does embracing trees help?

(*A Closer Look*, page 48)

Plants and Animals

India's climate supports rich vegetation. The Valley of Flowers in the western Himalayas has a carpet of primulas, dwarf rhododendrons, and irises that envelop the region for part of the year. The eastern region has luxuriant forests.

India is home to a variety of wild animals. Elephants in large numbers roam the forests in the state of Tamil Nadu, as do several species of deer and antelope. Two of the big cats, the tiger and the leopard, are found in the wild, although a third, the cheetah, has disappeared from the subcontinent. Thousands of lions once lived in the country; today, they number only about four hundred. Because of dwindling numbers, Assam's one-horned rhinoceros is now a protected species. To conserve wildlife, India has established game parks across the country.

Above: Sikkim, in the eastern Himalayas, has about four thousand species of flowering plants, including many types of rare orchids.

Left: Elephants play an important role in temple and palace ceremonies.

PROJECT TIGER

Many British officials claim they shot about a hundred tigers during their stay in India; others claim they killed as many as three hundred. Whatever the numbers, killing the animal for sport and money has led to a significant decline in India's tiger population. Project Tiger was launched to prevent the situation from worsening.

(A Closer Look, page 66)

History

Early History

Archaeological evidence suggests human activity in India between 400,000 and 200,000 B.C. Not much, however, was recorded between then and the rise of the Indus Valley Civilization in 3000 B.C., one of the earliest and most extensive civilizations in the world. By 1700 B.C., this civilization was in decline. Indo-Aryans from Iran invaded India soon after and established their base of power in what is now Delhi.

The Kings and Their Kingdoms

Alexander of Macedon, called Alexander the Great, crossed the Indus River into India in 326 B.C. and established several Greek settlements in the Punjab. His invasion was significant because it brought India in contact with lands to the west.

In 325 B.C., Chandragupta became the first king of the Maurya dynasty and, on Alexander's death, took control of the Greek settlements. Chandragupta extended his influence over parts of modern Afghanistan and much of northern and central India. He was succeeded by his son and later his grandson, Ashoka (269–232 B.C.). After Ashoka, the Mauryas continued to rule for half a century. They were followed by various dynasties: the Sungas, Karvas, and Guptas. The Guptas were the dominant power in the fourth and fifth centuries A.D.

Muslims started invading India in the tenth century. Around A.D. 1000, Mahmud of Ghazni, Afghanistan, began a series of raids into India. By 1026, he overran the Punjab but did not attempt to occupy the land. He wanted only gold, jewels, and slaves. Muslim raids resumed in the late twelfth century when Muhammad Ghauri invaded northern India. In 1206, a Muslim sultanate, called the Delhi Sultanate, was established in Delhi. The first sultan of the Slave Dynasty was Qutb-ud-din Aibak, who had been a slave of Muhammad Ghauri. He was succeeded by Iltutmish (1211–1236), Raziya (1236–1240), and Balban (1266–1287). During the period A.D. 850–1279, the Cholas, who were independent of the Delhi Sultanate, ruled central India. Farther south, a Hindu king ruled the kingdom of Vijayanagar, while the Marathas controlled the west.

Above: **King Ashoka converted from Hinduism to Buddhism and built pillars with Buddhist beliefs carved on them. They were erected in every important town. The symbol of lions at the top of Ashokan pillars is the emblem of the Indian government.**

In 1398, Timur (Tamerlane), a Turkic conqueror, led an invasion to overrun the Delhi Sultanate. The Sayyid and Lodi dynasties followed. Babur, King of Farghana (now in Uzbekistan), invaded India in 1524 and established the Mughal Empire. By the time Babur died in 1550, his domain covered most of the subcontinent. His son Humayun ruled next, followed by Humayun's son, Akbar. The Mughal Empire's decline began with Akbar's son, Jahangir.

Europeans Arrive

Portuguese navigator Vasco da Gama landed with his fleet at Calicut in 1498, restoring a link between Europe and the East that had existed several centuries earlier. The Dutch, French, and British soon followed. In 1608, the first British East India Company ship arrived in India. As central power in India declined, the company extended its control. In 1686, it declared war on the Mughal Empire. Robert Clive, governor of Madras (now Chennai) from 1755 to 1760 and governor of Calcutta from 1764 to 1767, was one of the people responsible for creating the British Empire in India.

Below: **The site of the first Portuguese landing in India.**

British Raj

Indian soldiers, called sepoys, working for the East India Company rebelled in 1857. The rebellion, called the Indian Mutiny by the British and the First War of Independence by the Indians, alarmed Britain and almost put an end to British rule. The sepoys declared the Mughal king Bahadur Shah the emperor of India, but the British exiled him to Burma, officially ending Mughal rule. In 1858, the British parliament transferred power from the East India Company to the British Crown, and a secretary of state aided by a council governed India. Subsequently, the governor general of India became the viceroy and was answerable to the British cabinet.

Several policy changes were initiated after the 1857 uprising. The legislative council was remodeled to include six Indians. Although these were Indian princes and members of the landed gentry, the inclusion was significant because it marked the first Indian participation in government. Princes who had stood by the British during the uprising were also rewarded.

The period 1858–1905 marked the high point of British rule in India. They built an extensive railway system, introduced an effective postal system, established modern industry, dug canals, averted famines, and introduced their education system.

Left: **The pretext for the Indian Mutiny (1857–1858) was the introduction of the new Enfield rifle. The sepoys believed that the grease lubricating the cartridges had cow and pig fat. The Hindus (who do not eat beef because they consider cows sacred) and Muslims (who do not eat pork because they consider pigs dirty) were outraged. When the sepoys refused to use the cartridges, they were jailed. Their angry comrades then shot their British officers and marched to Delhi. The British reacted with firepower.**

Sowing the Seeds of Unrest

The British education system gave rise to an educated middle class, but all classes of Indians soon realized that the rulers were not concerned about their interests. Modern Indian nationalism took root, and the Indian National Congress was formed in 1885. In both 1909 and 1919, reforms were introduced that gave Indians a share in the government. In the 1920s, prominent leaders, such as Mahatma Gandhi and Jawaharlal Nehru, led the nationalist movement. In the 1930s, the Muslim League also increased its political activities.

In 1943, Subhas Chandra Bose, an Indian revolutionary, with the help of the Japanese, launched the Indian National Army (INA) in Singapore. The INA conducted a military campaign for the liberation of India, but it collapsed after Japan was defeated in World War II. In 1946, the British granted independence to India. Several efforts at negotiation failed because the INA and the Muslim League, which wanted a separate state for the Muslims, could not agree on the future administration of the country. Violence between Hindus and Muslims increased.

Above: **The British in India before India's independence on August 15, 1947.**

GANDHI

Gandhi is credited with having gained independence for India. His method was unique because it was totally nonviolent. Trained as a lawyer, Gandhi later became a politician. Many Indians, whatever their religion or caste, respected him and still do even today.
(A Closer Look, page 52)

Independence and India Today

Lord Louis Mountbatten, who came to India as viceroy in March 1947, worked out a solution: India would be free from British rule but divided into a secular India and a Muslim Pakistan. The idea was accepted, and India gained independence on August 15, 1947. However, widespread violence and riots broke out in the two countries. People left in droves; millions lost their lives.

Jawaharlal Nehru became the first prime minister of India, and although the resettlement of refugees from Pakistan took several years, he brought the riots under control by the end of 1947. Almost half of the new India consisted of about six hundred princely states. Although they had been semi-independent under the British, they now agreed to join either India or Pakistan. On January 26, 1950, India became a democratic republic.

The presence of so many ethnic groups in India means that separatist movements arise across the country now and then. Although the Nehru-Gandhi dynasty ruled India for most of the post-independence era, over the years, their party, the Congress Party, became corrupt and lost the faith of the people. Other parties gained in strength. A series of coalition governments followed. In 1998, India came under the rule of a coalition government headed by Prime Minister Atal Behari Vajpayee.

MOTHER TERESA

Born in Yugoslavia in 1910, Mother Teresa came to India to care for the poor and needy. After becoming an Indian citizen, she founded the Missionaries of Charity in 1950. In 1979, she received the Nobel Peace Prize. She died in 1997.

Below: **Thousands crossed the new border during the partition of India.**

Akbar (1542–1605)

Abu-ul-Fath Jalal-ud-Din Muhammad Akbar was the greatest of India's Mughal emperors. At the beginning of his rule, his realm stretched from the Punjab to the area around Delhi. He gradually expanded his territory. Akbar did away with governmental practices that discriminated against non-Muslims. He respected Hindu sentiments and made the slaughter of cows illegal. He also abolished the tax on pilgrims and the tax that non-Muslims paid in lieu of military service. A great patron of the arts, Akbar duly awarded poets, musicians, and scholars for their works.

Subhas Chandra Bose (1897–1945)

Also called Netaji, Subhas Chandra Bose led an Indian national force against Western powers during World War II. After graduating from college in 1919, he went to the University of Cambridge in England to prepare for the Indian Civil Service. In 1921, after learning about the nationalist struggles back home, he left for India. In July, 1943, Bose became leader of the Indian independence movement in East Asia. He formed a strong army consisting of people from Japanese-occupied Southeast Asia. In October, he proclaimed the establishment of a provisional, independent Indian government. His Indian National Army, together with Japanese troops, advanced to Rangoon, and from there, overland into India. His army, however, was eventually defeated. Bose died a few days after the Japanese surrender in August 1945.

Subhas
Chandra
Bose

Lord Louis Mountbatten (1900–1979)

The last viceroy of India, Mountbatten's career involved extensive naval commands, the diplomatic negotiation of independence for India and Pakistan, and the highest military positions. As viceroy of India from March to August 1947, he administered the transfer of power from Britain to the newly independent nations of India and Pakistan at the partition of the subcontinent on August 15, 1947. As governor general of India from August 1947 to June 1948, he helped persuade the Indian princes to merge their states into either India or Pakistan.

Lord Louis
Mountbatten

Government and the Economy

Government

India consists of twenty-five states and seven centrally administered areas called union territories. New Delhi became the new capital in 1912 and today has become part of the larger city of Delhi. It is the seat of the union government and the president, prime minister, and almost all arms of the administration.

India's parliamentary system is modeled on the British one, in which the prime minister, aided by his or her cabinet, is the head of government. The president is the head of state. Parliament consists of a lower house called the Lok Sabha (House of the People) and an upper house called the Rajya Sabha (Council of States). Members of the Lok Sabha are elected for five-year terms by citizens aged eighteen and over from the various constituencies. Members of the Rajya Sabha represent their states and are elected by the state legislatures for six-year terms.

JAMMU AND KASHMIR

Jammu and Kashmir is the only state in India with a Muslim majority. Hindus, who make up 30 percent of the population, are mainly concentrated in and around Jammu. Pakistan and even China claim parts of Kashmir.

(A Closer Look, page 58)

Below: **Parliament House in New Delhi.**

NEHRU-GANDHI DYNASTY

The Nehru-Gandhi family dominated Indian politics from 1947 to 1991. Jawaharlal Nehru, his daughter, Indira Gandhi, and her son Rajiv all held the post of prime minister of India. In 1998, Rajiv's wife, Italian-born Sonia, became president of the Congress Party.

(A Closer Look, page 62)

Left: The Supreme Court in New Delhi.

The States

The states have a political system similar to that at the center. Each has a governor as head of state; a chief minister, aided by a council of ministers, as head of government; and a unicameral or bicameral legislature. The people elect the members of the lower house, the Vidhan Sabha, while local bodies elect the members of the upper house, the Vidhan Parishad.

The Indian National Congress, which played an important role in India's freedom movement, dominated Indian politics for the first few decades after the country's independence. Since the 1970s, many other political parties have emerged, and, today, if no party has a clear majority in the elections, the state in question may have a coalition government.

The Judicial System

The judicial system consists of the federal high court, the state high courts, and the local and district courts. These are headed by the Supreme Court, which has the right to rule on the constitutionality of laws passed by parliament. The Supreme Court also hears cases from the state courts.

PANCHAYAT RAJ

Indian states are divided into districts, each administered by a senior government official. To help the village communities participate in development planning, many forms of *panchayat raj* (puhn-CHA-yat RAHJ), or government by a council of community elders, were introduced, but they did not catch on in all the states. In some cases, the rich dominated the panchayat raj. The government is now trying to introduce new measures to help states have more control over administration.

Economy

Early Indian leaders felt the best way to develop the country was by minimizing competition to prevent unemployment and a waste of capital. Tight government control was imposed over production, employment, and prices. Realizing the ineffectiveness of these measures, later governments began relaxing the controls. Now, there are several multinational companies doing business in India, and because of economic liberalization since 1991, there has been a surge in foreign investment in the country.

Agriculture

Since 1947, India has seen a decline in agricultural output. Reasons for the decline include the use of non-mechanized agricultural methods, irrigation problems, and complications caused by erratic weather conditions. The government, therefore, has launched the "Green Revolution," providing farmers with improved varieties of seeds, increased quantities of fertilizers, and irrigation facilities. As a result, food grain production has increased, and famines have ended.

India is the largest exporter of tea and spices. Tea is a major earner of foreign exchange. Other important crops include rice, wheat, sorghum, millet, jute, oilseed, raw cotton, coffee, cashew nuts, sugarcane, rubber, and tobacco.

TEA

Some people believe that tea came to India from China, while others believe it originated in India. Whatever its origin, India is the largest consumer, exporter, and producer of black tea.
(A Closer Look, page 72)

Left: **Agriculture accounts for about two-thirds of the Indian labor force.**

Industry

In the 1950s and 1960s, a large, diversified industrial base was established in India, and, today, the country is home to a sophisticated industrial structure. Major investments have been made in such industries as fertilizers, steel, machine tools, electric and non-electric machinery, and transportation equipment. The electronics and cement industries are also growing. Until the entry of the multinationals (companies with branches or subsidiaries in many countries) in the 1980s and 1990s, most of the large industries in India were either in the hands of the government or were run by families, such as the Tatas and Birlas.

Transportation: The Land and the Sky

Roads connect capitals, ports, and other important towns. State highways connect major towns in the states, major district roads connect district headquarters to important areas in the region, and minor district roads connect villages. For many years, the Indian government ran the country's only international airline, Air India, and the domestic airline, Indian Airlines. In 1981, a third government airline, Vayudoot, started flying to previously inaccessible places. The government has since ended its monopoly on air transportation.

Above: **Initially built to transport soldiers and military supplies in British-occupied India, the railways have, over time, played a vital role in the economic, industrial, and social development of the country. With over 1.7 million employees, Indian Railways is one of the world's biggest employers.**

People and Lifestyle

Sheer Diversity

Most present-day Indians are descended from the Dravidians, whose origins are unknown but who were the early inhabitants of the country. Some Indians, however, are descended from the many groups of people who later came to the subcontinent as traders, marauders, or conquerors. The Aryans, for example, are light-skinned people who came from central Asia and Europe. They invaded India over the centuries and drove the Dravidians toward the south. The people of the north and northwestern regions of Kashmir, Rajasthan, New Delhi, and the Punjab are taller and fairer than the Dravidians, and some have light-colored eyes. People from the northeastern states, with small eyes and high cheekbones, are of Mongol descent.

Tribal Groups

India has many tribal groups. Some of them are: the Adivasis of Bihar; the Negritos (who number only a few hundred) of the Andaman and Nicobar islands; the Bhils of western India; and the

OVERPOPULATION

India is the second most populous country in the world, next to China. Overpopulation is one of its major problems, with unemployment and food shortages just some of the effects. Although efforts by the government in recent years have decreased the rate of population growth, the country still has a long way to go before achieving the desired rate.
(A Closer Look, page 64)

Below: **A wedding in the Bhil tribe.**

Left: Most Indian women in towns and villages wear saris. A sari is a long piece of material wrapped around the body. However, the *salwar-kameez* (suhl-WAHR-kuh-MEEZ), worn by the two girls on the extreme left of the picture, and Western dress have caught on in the cities, especially among working women. Men usually wear shirts and trousers on fair summer days. They wear western-style jackets or sleeveless vests, known as Nehru jackets, in the winter.

Boros and Karbis of the northeast. Scattered along the western coast of Gujarat are the Siddis. They are descendants of Africans who were probably brought to India by Arab traders some five hundred years ago and were later sold to the Portuguese who occupied Goa. The descendants of Arabs who settled in India are called Moplahs. They live in the northern part of Kerala.

You Are What You Wear

Each region and ethnic group in India has its own distinct dress. People in Jammu and Kashmir wear cotton trousers with a woolen upper garment. Rajasthani women wear heavy skirts and short tunics, with a headscarf and heavy silver jewelry. The men wear frock-like tunics and narrow trousers.

Hindu women wear the *bindi* (BIN-dee), a dot on the forehead. Although traditionally red and worn only by married women, bindis now come in all colors, shapes, and sizes and are worn even by unmarried women. Red or white bindi-like spots along the length of the eyebrows beautify brides.

INDIAN TEXTILES

Indians love vibrant colors, and they demonstrate this best in their clothes. The sari, favored by many Indian women, has fascinated many travelers to India. Because it is not cut or tailored for any particular size, there is no need for alterations, and can be worn in a variety of ways. Indians can usually pinpoint the region a woman belongs to from the way she wears her sari.
(A Closer Look, page 56)

Family Life

Indians are generally family oriented. Many traditional families in cities and villages have as many as three generations living under the same roof. However, more and more men in rural areas are moving to the cities in search of work, and with new laws limiting land holdings, the extended family as a social unit is slowly giving way to the nuclear family.

Family members maintain close ties. Weddings and christenings are occasions for the extended family to get together and celebrate. The family network is equally supportive when misfortune strikes any of its members. When there is a death, all branches of the family gather to offer support and share the grief.

The Khasis of the northeast are a matrilinear society. In this community, the husband moves into his wife's home, and children carry their mother's clan name. Daughters rather than sons inherit ancestral property; thus, parents are more enthusiastic about having female rather than male babies.

Other than the Khasis, most Indian societies are patrilinear — the father is the head of the family and the laws of inheritance favor males. From this social structure came the dowry system, in

Above: **A middle-class Hindu family of four generations.**

Opposite: **A traditional Tamil Hindu wedding conducted by a priest. The bride and bridegroom take their vows before a fire.**

which women received gifts from their parents when they married. Over time, this system disintegrated. Potential grooms began requesting goods from the bride's parents and, in extreme cases, called off the wedding when demands were not met. Today, there is a trend, especially among the young and educated, to view a dowry as an unnecessary evil, and many are doing away with the giving and receiving of extravagant gifts for weddings.

Above: Girls with henna on their hands. American singer Madonna popularized henna in the West in her album *Ray of Light*, which was released in 1998.

Wedding Bells

A wedding is one of the most important family events. Siblings and other relatives make a special effort to attend, even traveling long distances to be part of the festivities. The feasting and merrymaking sometimes stretch to four or more days.

Women and children are enthusiastic participants. They attend the ceremony dressed in pretty outfits and jewelry. Most women, including the bride and sometimes the bridegroom, apply henna in beautiful designs on their hands and feet. Because marriage is viewed as a lifelong commitment sanctioned by God, divorce is taboo in Indian society. Hindu widows, as dictated by custom, usually dress in plain white saris and do not wear the bindi or jewelry. They are passive participants during weddings.

Education

Education is largely the responsibility of state governments. Different states have different curricula and examinations. In some schools, English or Hindi is taught as the first language and regional languages as the second; in others, the reverse is the norm. Some schools are affiliated with examination boards in New Delhi; others are part of their state's system.

Primary and secondary education take ten years, followed by two years in junior college and three to five years in college. Primary education at government-run schools is free until the fifth grade, as is education to the eighth grade in most states and union territories. In a few places, secondary education is also free.

The government has been making efforts in the last five decades to improve the country's literacy rate. Today, about 50 percent of the population is literate. The rate varies widely from state to state, but Kerala stands out for having a literacy rate of more than 90 percent. Yet, India's national literacy rate is still behind that of many developing countries, such as Vietnam (94 percent), Kenya (78 percent), and Rwanda (60 percent).

Above: **The school day usually begins with an assembly, where prayers are recited and important announcements for the day are made.**

Have Money, Will Study

The system of higher education in India favors those with money. Only those who can afford it go to college — the rest stop their education midway to find work. On the other hand, half the rural poor do not even have proper primary education, and many drop out of primary school before finishing.

India has 197 universities and about 5 million university students. It is difficult to finance such a large educational system. Institutions of higher learning continually suffer from shortages of funds. Despite these shortages, the country continues to turn out world-class doctors, engineers, and other professionals from the Indian Institutes of Technology, All India Institute of Medical Sciences, and other prestigious institutions. These schools admit only a small percentage of the brightest applicants every year.

India has made impressive strides in science and technology. It builds jet engines, designs computers, and has several plutonium reactors. The country is well represented in many international conferences and seminars on physics, statistics, economics, and medicine.

Below: **Cramming for major examinations is a way of life for students in many institutions.**

Religion

About 80 percent of Indians are Hindu. Hinduism, one of the oldest religions in the world, is more a way of life than a religion. It has no founder, and its basic beliefs can be interpreted in different ways. Hindus pray to many gods and goddesses. They believe these gods are different manifestations of one Supreme God, or Brahman.

The Caste System

Hindu society was traditionally divided into four castes based on occupation. They were the Brahmins, or priests; the Kshatriyas, or warriors; the Vaishyas, or traders; and the Sudras, or manual workers. The caste system gave order to life and laid down rules for conduct. Over time, however, the system gave rise to social evils, such as considering some people untouchables or outcastes.

Reaction to these evils, as well as to the other rituals of Hinduism, sparked a number of reform movements, such as the Brahmo Samaj and Arya Samaj. A popular offshoot of Hinduism is Jainism, founded in the sixth century B.C. by Mahavira. Its basic doctrine is nonviolence to all living creatures.

BUDDHA

Buddha's teachings have influenced many people in Asia. In the 1960s and early 1970s, Buddhism became popular in the West among young people who wanted new forms of religious expression. There are now a number of Buddhists in the West, among them Hollywood actor Richard Gere.
(A Closer Look, page 46)

Left: Visiting the temple is a daily ritual for some Hindus. Others go once a week.

HINDU DEITIES

According to the *Mahabharata*, a Hindu epic, there are 33,333 Hindu deities. Later sources, however, put the figure much higher. Some gods have several different forms, or incarnations, which probably account for their large numbers.
(A Closer Look, page 54)

Indians of Other Faiths

Muslims, the largest religious minority, form slightly more than 10 percent of the country's population. They are the descendants of either the Muslim clans that invaded India or Hindus who converted to Islam. Some converted to escape the rigidity imposed by the Hindu caste system. Others converted because of religious discrimination. Some Muslim rulers imposed high taxes on non-Muslims, while others, such as Mughal ruler Aurangzeb, pardoned criminals if they converted to Islam.

Sikhs form 2 percent of the population, and another 3 percent belong to different religions, such as Buddhism (which originated in India), Christianity, animism (practiced by some remote tribes, such as the Bhils, Gonds, and Santhals), and Zoroastrianism. The Zoroastrians who live in the area around Mumbai are known as Parsis. They are the descendants of Zoroastrians who fled Iran between the eighth and tenth centuries to escape religious persecution. Although a small community, the Parsis have made their mark in fields ranging from the arts (Zubin Mehta) to business (the Tata family). They are a close-knit community and rarely marry outside their faith.

Above: **Muslims at prayer in a mosque. India has the third largest population of Muslims in the world, after Indonesia and Pakistan. The government subsidizes their pilgrimage, called Haj, to Mecca and Medina.**

SIKHISM

This religion began in India in the late fifteenth century. Read about its founder and his nine successors, and find out where the holiest Sikh shrine is located.
(A Closer Look, page 68)

Language and Literature

Languages and Dialects

Hindi and English are the official languages of India. English, however, has less importance than Hindi. Most government communication is in these two languages or in a regional language. In addition to English and Hindi, the government recognizes seventeen other languages: Assamese, Bengali, Gujarati, Nepali, Manipuri, Konkani, Kannada, Kashmiri, Malayalam, Marathi, Oriya, Punjabi, Sanskrit, Sindhi, Tamil, Telugu, and Urdu. Apart from these languages, about 1,652 dialects are spoken in the country.

Most Indian languages and dialects are descended from the Aryan or Dravidian languages. Dravidian languages were used by the original inhabitants of India and include Kannada, Tamil,

Left: The press has enjoyed considerable freedom since India gained independence. Although newspapers appear in all the major languages, those in English are the most influential.

Telugu, and Malayalam. The Indo-Aryan languages evolved from Sanskrit, which subsequently fell into disuse because of its difficult grammar and pronunciation. Sanskrit now exists as the language of Hindu ritual and worship.

Sindhi is the only Indian language that does not belong to any particular state because Sindh became part of Pakistan during independence. Nepali, the only official foreign language apart from English, is now recognized as an Indian language because the Darjeeling district in West Bengal is inhabited mostly by immigrants from Nepal.

When Muslims ruled India, they made Persian the court language, but they wanted a language that the common person on the street could understand. Urdu evolved to fill this role. Over time, Urdu became popular, and some outstanding literature, particularly poetry, was written in that language.

Above: In 1913, Rabindranath Tagore (1861–1941) won the Nobel Prize for Literature for the English version of his *Gitanjali* ("Song Offering"). Tagore was also an eminent painter and a gifted composer.

Ancient Texts

The earliest known Indian literary works are the *Vedas*, the ancient Hindu texts of hymns and chants used in Hindu rituals. The *Upanishads*, the most important part of the Vedas, contain philosophies and spiritual truths. Some Hindu epics present the philosophy of the *Upanishads* in the form of stories. The most well-known epics are the *Ramayana* and the *Mahabharata*.

Poets and Writers

The great poets of the last few centuries include Mirza Ghalib (1797–1869). In his writing, he praised God but questioned the misery he saw around him. In 1914, Sarojini Naidu (1879–1949) was elected a fellow of England's Royal Society of Literature.

One of the greatest Indian writings is Kalidasa's drama *Shakuntala* from the fifth century A.D. Tulsidas's *Ramcharitmanas* ("Sacred Lake of the Acts of Ram") is a poem that expresses devotion to the Hindu god Ram. It is believed to have replaced the cult for the god Krishna in northern India with the cult of Ram. In recent years, many books by Indians writing in English have made their mark on the world. These include Salman Rushdie's *The Satanic Verses*, banned in some countries for its controversial content; Vikram Seth's *A Suitable Boy* (1993); and Arundhati Roy's *The God of Small Things* (1997), which won her the Booker Prize.

STORIES OF YESTERYEAR

The *Puranas* (puh-RA-nahs) are collections of short, simple stories that educate people about Hinduism. The stories were passed down from grandmothers to their grandchildren, and by village priests to the common folk. The *Panchatantra* (PUHN-cher-TUN-tra) is another rich source of stories. These stories, using human and animal characters, teach moral values. Some believe the Panchatantra inspired Aesop's fables.

Arts

Of Ancient Forts and More

Ancient kings built forts all across the country. Most are now in ruins, but Shah Jahan's Red Fort in Delhi and the Amber Fort in Jaipur are still in good condition.

The Gwalior and Chittor forts are good examples of Hindu architecture. When Sultan Alauddin Khalji of the Delhi Sultanate attacked the Chittor Fort in 1303, the Rajput women inside preferred death to dishonor and jumped into a fire. This heroic deed is the subject of many folk songs in Rajasthan.

The stupas of Sanchi and Sarnath are among the earliest examples of Buddhist architecture. Their walls and columns are decorated with elaborate images that detail the life of Buddha. Ellora in western India has magnificent temples. Of these, the Kailashanatha Temple, which is 96 feet (29 m) high and 165 feet (50 m) long, was excavated out of a single rock. Other well-known temples are in Mount Abu, Madurai, and Kanchipuram.

AJANTA AND ELLORA CAVES

The Ajanta Caves contain Buddhist temples and monasteries, with frescoes depicting Buddhist legends. The nearby Ellora temples are popular for their exquisite carvings and sculptures of Hindu gods and mythological figures.
(A Closer Look, page 44)

Left: **The Mughals built the Red Fort in the seventeenth century. The fort gets its name from its red sandstone walls.**

Muslim and British Architecture

Muslim mosques and tombs, with their minarets and domes, are a blend of Persian, Egyptian, Syrian, and central Asian styles. In the seventeenth century, Shah Jahan built the Taj Mahal in Agra for his wife, Mumtaz Mahal. The mausoleum is the best-known Muslim architectural masterpiece.

Other important Muslim monuments are the Qutub Minar and the tomb of Ghiyas-ud-din Tughlaq in New Delhi, and the Chand Minar at Daulatabad. The Gol Gumbaz in Bijapur, 131 feet (40 m) across and the largest dome in the world, is an acoustic wonder. If you whisper along the perimeter, someone on the other side of the dome can hear you clearly.

The British left their mark on churches, residences, and office buildings across the country. Victoria Memorial in Calcutta, which opened to the public in 1921, is a museum that tells the story of the British Empire in India. British architect Sir Edwin Lutyens drew the city plan for New Delhi. Now a far cry from its original plan, this city has expanded in every direction. Lutyens also designed the Viceroy's House, now known as Rashtrapati Bhawan, the home of the president.

Above: **The Maharaja's Palace in Mysore, with its ivory and gold throne, was built in 1897.**

TAJ MAHAL

Regarded as one of the wonders of the world, the Taj Mahal is the ultimate symbol of love. It was built by Mughal king Shah Jahan in the seventeenth century and is situated beside the Yamuna River. The mausoleum is a favorite destination for Indians and tourists.

(A Closer Look, page 70)

A Different Beat

Indian classical music has two schools, Hindustani and Carnatic. Hindustani music, the music of northern India, is influenced by Arabic and Iranian music, as a result of the Muslim invasions of the twelfth and thirteenth centuries. Carnatic music, the music of southern India, evolved from Hindu traditions thousands of years ago.

Both Hindustani and Carnatic music are based on *ragas* (RA-gah), or set compositions of five to seven notes. The *tanpura* (TAHN-poo-rah), a four-stringed instrument, usually accompanies vocal performances. Today, vocalists like Ustad Bade Ghulam Ali Khan keep the classical tradition in vocal music alive. Besides the tanpura, another important instrument used in Indian classical music is the *sitar* (si-TAHR).

In recent years, the influence of Western music and instruments on mainstream Indian music has been quite dramatic. The reverse is also true to some extent. Some interesting partnerships have sprung out of this mutual influence and appreciation, such as that between popular Indian singer Asha Bhosle and British singer Boy George.

Opposite: Manipuri is smooth and graceful and technically easier to master than other Indian dance forms. It is indigenous to Manipur and became popular throughout India in 1917 when Rabindranath Tagore brought manipuri dance teachers to his Visva-Bharati University at Santiniketan.

Indian Dance

Traditional Indian dance falls into two main groups, classical and folk. The six classical dance forms, bharatanatyam, kathak, kathakali, kucipudi, manipuri, and orissi, follow rigid rules and involve intricate footwork, as well as stylized gestures and facial expressions. They take years of practice and dedication to master. Bharatanatyam was originally performed only by female temple dancers. It was not performed on stage for the public until 1930. Orissi, which is related to bharatanatyam in its basic pattern, is thrilling to watch because of the variety of jumps in the dance.

Folk dances, which are part of most celebrations, differ from one ethnolinguistic group to another. Some popular ones are the bhangra of the Punjab, the garba of Gujarat, and the bihu of Assam. In recent years, bhangra music and dance have gained an international following.

Government-controlled television and radio networks present classical dance and music programs and have been successful in popularizing them. The government has also established institutions to nurture the various art forms.

Above: **A typical bharatanatyam dancer in all her finery. This dance is prevalent in southern India.**

Leisure and Festivals

The Power of Television

Most Indians live in villages, where people tend to the fields from dawn till dusk. Leisure for them means chatting with friends and neighbors in the evening or watching television if they own one. Watching television is also a popular pastime in the cities. In 1972, when television first came to India, there were only two channels, and both were sponsored by the government.

Since 1990, however, cable has brought dozens of international channels into the homes of many Indians, who now have a direct taste of Western culture and values. Many are influenced by what they see. For instance, beauty titles are now seen as a means to fame and fortune, where the winner must possess not only beauty but also brains. Many young educated women no longer shun these titles. With the support of parents and friends, they take part in beauty pageants. The results speak for themselves: in the 1990s alone, India garnered one Miss Universe title and two Miss World titles.

Below: **Snakes and Ladders is a favorite pastime among children, as is playing computer games for those who can afford them.**

A Mode of Escapism

Many Indians, especially the less privileged, find watching movies, with good-looking stars, catchy song and dance numbers, and a happy ending, a form of escapism from the drudgery of their own lives. The Mumbai film industry, often compared to Hollywood, is called "Bollywood," a name that offends some Indians because it implies an imitation of Hollywood.

Genius at Work

Some Indian works, such as the movies of Satyajit Ray, have gained critical acclaim from international audiences. A motion-picture director and writer, Ray put Indian cinema on the world stage. His movie *Pather Panchali*, completed in 1955, was a success in Bengal and in the West, following a major award at the 1956 Cannes International Film Festival. By 1959, he completed two other movies of the trilogy, *Aparajito* and *Apur Sanasr*. He produced many other movies. In 1992, Ray was presented with a Lifetime Achievement Oscar for his contributions to the Indian and the international movie industries.

Above: Nowhere in the world are movies more popular than in India. The country has the most prolific film industry in the world, churning out about eight hundred films yearly. The proliferation of videos in the cities, however, has affected attendance at cinemas. Rural folk, on the other hand, still enjoy a night out at the movies.

Outdoor Games

Kite flying is a popular sport, especially in early spring. When there is a lull in agricultural activity, people in the north engage in tugs-of-war, bull races, and wrestling contests. Boat racing in Kerala and *gatka* (GAT-kah) in Punjab are also popular outdoor sports. The gatka is a stick about 4 feet (1.2 m) long with leather hand-guards. Two opponents fence with the gatka, and the player who touches an opponent's body the most number of times is the winner. The popular Indian games *kabaddi* (kuh-BAD-di) and *kho-kho* (KHOH-KHOH) are modified versions of tag.

Cricket: A Passion

The British brought cricket to India, and the Indians made it their own. If soccer has a regional following, cricket has a grip on the entire nation. Pakistan and India are traditional rivals. Emotions run so high that, for a few years, matches were played on neutral ground. One well-known Indian cricketer, K. S. Ranjitsinhji, played for England from 1896 to 1902. In 1899, he became the first player to reach 3,000 runs in an English season. His son, K. S.

Above: **Young men practice cricket in neighborhood parks throughout the year. They and other fans of the national cricket team never miss cricket games shown on television.**

Duleepsinhji, played for England from 1929 to 1931. More recent players, Sunil Gavaskar and Kapil Dev, are in the *Guinness Book of Records*, the former for the most runs in test cricket and the latter for the largest number of wickets by a bowler. Ravi Shastri holds the record for scoring the fastest runs.

Hockey and Other Sports

Between 1928 and 1956, India won six consecutive Olympic gold medals for field hockey. It also won gold medals at the 1964 Tokyo Olympics and the 1980 Moscow Olympics.

Soccer is popular in the northeastern states of Bengal, Assam, and Orissa. The excitement starts weeks before the season, and matches are emotionally charged. There are three major soccer teams, Mohammedan Sporting, East Bengal, and Mohan Bagan. Tennis is now gaining popularity in India, thanks to the efforts of Leander Paes and Mahesh Bhupathi. Bhupathi won the French Open mixed doubles title in 1997.

Adventure sports, such as sailing and white-water rafting, are beginning to catch the fancy of India's young people. Billiards, despite a limited following, has produced some world champions, such as Wilson Jones, S. Aleem, and Geet Sethi.

KABADDI

Kabaddi is an Indian game that combines elements of rugby and wrestling. People in the rural parts of India enjoy playing it because the game is simple and requires no equipment. Kabaddi is also popular in Bangladesh, Japan, and other countries.

(A Closer Look, page 60)

Left: The British army is credited for popularizing the game of field hockey in India. In the 1928 Olympic Games, India won the gold medal despite competing in the sport for the first time. In the late 1940s, Pakistan challenged India's domination of the game. Currently, countries such as the Netherlands, Australia, and Pakistan have better world rankings in field hockey than India.

The Two Eids

The ninth month of the Muslim calendar, known as Ramadan, is a month of strict fasting between sunrise and sunset. Eid-ul-Fitr marks the end of the fasting month. Every Muslim celebrates the festival with great enthusiasm. The day begins with prayers at the mosque. Women pray at home and cook special dishes for the celebration. Between early morning and noon prayers, Muslims recite the Eid prayer. As soon as it is over, they embrace and wish each other a happy and auspicious Eid (Eid Mubarak). Eid-uz-Zuha, which falls two months and nine days later, commemorates Abraham's bid to sacrifice his son Ishmael. Allah, by a miracle, substituted a ram. This festival is celebrated by slaughtering an animal, and the meat is donated to the poor.

Color Me Beautiful

Holi, celebrated on the day after the full moon in early March, is a favorite among children. It is a chance for them to get as messy as they want without anyone objecting. In the streets, people, whether friends or strangers, throw colored water at each other.

Below: On Holi, children use water guns to spray their friends and smear each other's faces with brightly colored powders. Adults, too, take part in the fun.

Holi originally celebrated the harvest and the fertility of the land, but, along the way, it came to symbolize a Hindu legend. A king hated his son, Prahlad, who worshiped the god Vishnu. He tried to kill the boy several times but failed. Finally, his sister, Holika, who was said to be immune to burning, offered to sit in a fire with the boy. Instead of Prahlad, Holika burned to death.

Flowers, Damsels, and Boat Races

Celebrated in August or September, Onam — the main festival of Kerala — involves ten days of feasting, boat races, and merrymaking. According to legend, the god Vishnu ousted King Mahabali from his kingdom. King Mahabali was so attached to his subjects that he asked permission to visit them once a year. Onam is the day when King Mahabali pays his people a visit. Ten days before Onam, *pookkalam* (POO-kuh-lum), or floral decorations, are put on every home. One of the highlights of the festivities is a boat race, with oars flashing in and out of the water to strains of music. In the evening, young girls dance around traditional brass lamps.

Above: **Young girls in bright outfits strike a pretty pose beside a *pookkalam* during Onam in Kerala.**

FESTIVAL OF LIGHTS

Hindus across India celebrate Diwali in their own special way. Some light lamps at night; others visit friends and relatives for tea, lunch, or dinner. Children receive gifts of money and sample a variety of mouthwatering Indian sweets that are usually forbidden by adults on other days.

(A Closer Look, page 50)

Food

At the Mercy of the Weather

India is an agricultural economy, so people's eating habits center around the crops they grow and the animals they raise. The staple food in the north is wheat; in the south, it is rice. This distinction, however, is no longer as clear as it once used to be. During the last fifty years of British rule and the first twenty years of independence, there were severe food shortages in the country. The distribution of grain to various parts of India was regulated, depending on which cereal was available. Often, it happened to be rice. So, now, people across India consume both rice and wheat. Rice is served boiled, steamed, or as shallow-fried pancakes. Wheat is used to make different kinds of bread.

The typical Indian lunch or dinner consists of one or two vegetables cooked in oil and spices, lentils, yogurt, and rice or breads, such as *chapati* (cha-PAH-ti). Chapatis are round and flat

Opposite: *Paan* **(PAHN) is a betel leaf smeared with catechu, lime paste, and fragrant essences and wrapped around shredded betel nut, cardamom, aniseed, and other ingredients. Paan is often eaten at the end of a traditional Indian meal.**

Left: **A delicious Indian meal of rice, breads, vegetables, and meat. Most people use their right hand to eat, especially if they are having bread or** *dosai* **(THOH-sei). Eating rice with the hand or with a fork and spoon is a matter of personal preference and lifestyle.**

and look somewhat like tortillas. They are best eaten hot, when they are puffed up and soft. For special occasions, chapatis are replaced by *paratha* (pur-RAH-tha), which are fried and stuffed with meat or vegetables, or simply fried with egg on them.

Cooking in the cities is usually done on a gas stove. A heavy flat pan is used for making chapati, while flat- or round-bottomed pots are used for lentils and curries. In the villages, cooking is generally done on small earthen stoves fueled by charcoal or cowdung cakes.

For Those with a Sweet Tooth

During major Hindu festivals, friends and relatives exchange sweets. North Indian sweets are largely milk based. Milk is boiled until it becomes a solid mass. It is then mixed with a variety of nuts, dried fruit, and flavorings to make *burfee* (BUHR-fee) and other sweets. Bengali sweets, such as *shondesh* (SHON-daish) and *roshogolla* (raw-shoh-GOL-lah), made from cottage cheese, are very popular. In the south, *paks* (PAHKS) are made from a mixture of lentil flour, milk, and nuts.

SNACK TIME!

Some popular snacks are *samosas* (suh-MOW-sahs); *bhujia* (BHU-jiah), or spicy lentil vermicelli; and *chaat* (CHAHT). In the summer, sherbets and fruit juices are in great demand. A traditional summer cooler is *thandaai* (thuhn-DAEE), which is made by grinding together almonds, cardamoms, black pepper, fennel seeds, sugar, and rose petals and creaming the paste through a strainer with iced water.

A CLOSER LOOK AT INDIA

This section is about some of the facets of Indian society that make the country unique. From the ancient Ajanta and Ellora caves to the breathtaking Taj Mahal, India's cultural heritage enriches any visitor to the country. India's allure also stems from its heterogeneous society, which unfortunately, is also a source of many of the country's problems. Hindu-Muslim disagreements, for instance, have cost thousands of lives. On the bright side, the existence of different religious groups means a rich culture and

Opposite: **The Qutub Minar complex in New Delhi dates from around 1200** A.D. **Its minaret at 278 feet (85 m) was, for many years, the world's tallest.**

many festivals to celebrate throughout the year. One such festival is Diwali. Read about the legend behind Diwali, and find out why Hindus light oil lamps at night during this festival. Turn a few more pages, and you will learn why the Hindu god Ganesha has an elephant's head on a human body.

In a country of vast forests, scenic landscapes, and wild animals, India's development has, over the years, taken its toll on the environment. Read about Sunderlal Bahuguna, Valmik Thapar, and the women in Uttarkhand and their efforts to save what remains of the country's wildlife and vegetation.

Above: **Colorfully decorated pumpkins bring smiles to these boys' faces.**

Ajanta and Ellora Caves

Sighted by Chance

The Ajanta and Ellora caves, a group of cave shrines carved out of rock, are in Maharashtra in western India. Some of the Ajanta caves date from the second century B.C., while the Ellora caves date back to the fourth century B.C. Because the caves were buried under a thick blanket of jungle and creepers, only the local Bhil tribe knew of their existence. In 1819, however, a group of British officers on a tiger hunt spotted them and brought the caves' obscurity to an abrupt end.

The thirty caves at Ajanta depict the story of Buddhism from 200 B.C. to A.D. 650. Monks excavated and painted the caves with murals that depict the life of Buddha and Buddhist fables. Sometime in the seventh century, the site was abandoned because of the growing popularity of nearby Ellora and the resurgence of Hinduism. By the eighth century, the complex was deserted and forgotten.

Below: **Students on a trip to the Ajanta caves. Ajanta has beautiful paintings and excellent sculptures.**

Inside Ellora: Traveling Back in Time

The thirty-four Ellora caves have elaborate facades and interiors. Carved with hand tools between A.D. 350 and 700, the monasteries and rock temples are among the most important historical monuments in India.

Cave 32 has two levels: the lower level is incomplete, but the upper level contains intricate sculptures and carvings. On the ceiling is a massive carving of a lotus, as well as elaborate paintings. An icon of Mahavira, the founder of Jainism, can also be found in this cave.

The centerpiece at Ellora is the Kailashanatha Temple in cave 16. It is 165 feet (50 m) long and 96 feet (29 m) high and took over a century to complete. This architectural wonder is a mass of rock cut out from the hillside and later sculpted into a temple. The cave's assembly hall, measuring 66 feet (20 m) by 55 feet (17 m), has a sanctum for the symbol of the god Shiva. Inside the temple, paintings portray Shiva's myths. One of them represents the struggle between good and evil. There are also carvings of Ganesha, Durga, and other gods and goddesses, as well as scenes from the *Ramayana* and *Mahabharata* epics.

Above: **Carvings at Ellora depict Buddhist, Jain, and Hindu faiths.**

Buddha

Buddha (563–483 B.C.) was born Siddhartha Gautama but was later given the title Buddha, which means "the Enlightened One." Saddened by the sorrow, suffering, and death around him, Buddha renounced his worldly ties at a young age and hoped to find some religious understanding and release from the human condition. He first tried the ascetic way of self-inflicted suffering but was not satisfied. He then sat under a pipul tree at Bodh Gaya in Bihar and resolved not to leave the spot until he saw the inner meaning of life. After a long spell of meditation, he achieved enlightenment, or ultimate understanding.

Opposite: Devotees at a Buddhist temple in Himachal Pradesh.

The Four Noble Truths

Buddha taught his followers a path between a life of worldly pleasures and a life of self-denial. He preached that nirvana, or salvation from sorrow, lay in detaching oneself from worldly things. He taught the following Four Noble Truths: (1) life is full of suffering and disappointment; (2) suffering is a result of man's

Below: Young monks surround a mandala, or a symbolic diagram, which is used in performing sacred rites. It is also used as an instrument of meditation.

desires for pleasure, power, and continued existence; (3) to stop suffering and disappointment, one must stop desiring; and (4) the way to stop desiring and suffering is the Noble Eightfold Path of right views, right intention, right speech, right action, right livelihood, right effort, right awareness, and right concentration.

Ashoka: Great Patron of Buddhism

Historically, the best-known follower of Buddha's teachings was Ashoka, the great Maurya king. In 250 B.C., he went on a pilgrimage to Lumbini, Buddha's birthplace, and marked the place with a great stone pillar. In Bodh Gaya, he built a simple shrine to mark the spot where Buddha attained enlightenment. The Mahabodhi Temple, which later became an important place of pilgrimage, replaced the shrine in the second century A.D.

Below: A statue of Buddha, the founder of Buddhism.

The temple was expanded and renovated several times. In 1877, Mindon Min, the last Burmese king, sent a mission to Bodh Gaya to renovate the temple and bring it back to life. He wanted to build a monastery and provide accommodations for pilgrims. When the Anglo-Burmese War broke out soon after, the mission returned. The British decided to complete the task but shipped off some of the finest Buddha statues and antiquities to London. Bodh Gaya today is a small village that has grown around the Mahabodhi Temple.

Embracing Trees

Rural people, especially those living in the hills, depend on forests for food, fodder, and fuel. Forests also stabilize the soil and water resources. Over the years, many forests have been destroyed for commerce and industry. Today, forests cover only 23 percent of India compared to 40 percent a century ago. Villagers who depend on forests for a livelihood have had to search for alternative sources of income.

Putting Up a Fight

In the 1970s, local villagers, particularly women, in the Himalayan region of Uttarkhand organized a nonviolent movement to protect their forests. In 1973, when bulldozers and lumberjacks came to fell the trees and clear the land, the women embraced the trees and shielded them. They tied sacred threads on the trees as an expression of their promise to protect them. The movement spread throughout India and became known as the Chipko movement. In Hindi, *chipko* means "embrace."

Opposite: **Sunderlal Bahuguna is now campaigning actively in Uttar Pradesh to stop the construction of the Tehri Dam over the Ganges. He and other Chipko activists fear the dam will uproot trees and cause massive flooding. To protest against the dam, he fasted for seventy-four days in 1996 and eleven days in June 1997.**

Below: **Extensive logging has destroyed vast forests in India. The country lost 31.2 million acres (12.6 million hectares) between 1950 and 1982.**

48

CRIES HEARD

In 1965, women in Tehri Garhwal launched an anti-alcohol movement. Their husbands threatened to throw them out of their homes, but they stood their ground. Movements such as this one inspired the women in Tehri Garhwal to go ahead with the Chipko movement. Their cries were finally heard. In 1980, Indira Gandhi banned the commercial felling of trees above 3,283 feet (1,000 m) for fifteen years and had new trees planted to provide fuel, fodder, and food. The ban was successful. Today, both men and women living in the hills, as well as others, are still active in their campaign to prevent future forest clearings.

The women tried to convince forest contractors and government officials that clearing forests had caused floods in 1970 and droughts in 1972 and 1973. Raising livestock, finding firewood, and providing food for their families became difficult. Men migrated to the plains to look for work, while women tilled the land and cared for their children. Women were thus the main victims of deforestation.

The Mahatma of India's Forests

An important figure in the Chipko movement is Sunderlal Bahuguna, revered by many Indians as "the Mahatma of India's forests." In 1982 and 1983, he walked 3,025 miles (4,867 km) through the Himalayas. He saw the ecological and social devastation brought about by development projects and submitted his findings to the United Nations. The report attracted the attention of local officials and spread the Chipko message to other parts of India, including Himachal Pradesh in the north, Rajasthan in the west, Bihar in the east, Karnataka in the south, and the Vindhyas in central India.

FLOODS IN INDIA

Every year, monsoon rains and deforestation cause widespread flooding on the eastern and western coasts of India, as well as states inland. The 1998 floods were particularly devastating in Assam, West Bengal, Uttar Pradesh, and other northeastern states. Houses were damaged, and people had to be evacuated to safety. Many also lost their lives.

Festival of Lights

Hindus all across India celebrate Diwali, or the Festival of Lights (literally meaning "rows of *deeps* (DEEPS)," or clay lamps). The festival, which falls some time in October or November, symbolizes the victory of good over evil. Hindus light deeps in their homes. They also set them adrift on rivers and streams. At night, fireworks light up the sky in a wonderful display of vibrant colors and shapes. Children like Diwali; they enjoy the fireworks and the general air of festivity on the days leading up to the festival. Some children even help their mothers make mouthwatering goodies to eat.

Left: Ram (center) and his wife, Sita (right), bless Hanuman, the monkey god. Ram's brother, Lakshman, is on the left. Diwali celebrates Ram's return to his kingdom.

Lights, Sweets, Company, and More!

Diwali commemorates Ram's return to his kingdom, Ayodhya, after fourteen years of exile. Ram was an incarnation of the Hindu god Vishnu, and his stories are well loved. The festival also marks the start of the Hindu new year. Hindus spring-clean and decorate the floors and walls of their houses with *rangoli* (rung-GOH-lee), or decorative designs. They draw the designs with plain or colored rice flour mixed in water. Prior to the festival, much time is spent choosing the right greeting cards to send friends and relatives. On the day of the festival, everyone wears new clothes, exchanges sweets, and takes food offerings to temples.

Above: **Diwali is an important day for businesses. It marks the beginning of their fiscal year. Accountants settle their companies' old accounts and open new books for good luck.**

Diwali lasts five days, although now, only the third day is celebrated on a big scale. On the first day, called the Dhanteras, Hindus worship Lakshmi, the goddess of wealth and prosperity. Wealth, never considered evil or undesirable in Indian culture, is believed to be a reward for good deeds done in a past life.

On the second day, Kali Chaudas, people worship Kali, the goddess of strength. The day is also known as Narak Chaturdasi. Legend has it that Narakasur, an evil king, abused his powers and imprisoned several young women. Lord Krishna and his wife, Satyabhama, killed the king and rescued the women. The day is remembered for the freedom people gained from Narakasur's tyranny.

The third day is Diwali itself. Lamps are lit outside homes and offices. Relatives and friends visit each other's homes for lunch or dinner. The merriment continues late into the night with special parties. Those who prefer the company of close friends gamble with them into the wee hours of the night. This custom has its origins in the games of dice played by Hindu gods Shiva and Parvati.

A Special Meaning for the Jains

Diwali has a very important meaning for the Jain community. It commemorates the death of Mahavira, the most recent Jain saint. They light lamps on this day to symbolize the light of holy knowledge that was extinguished after his death. The day after Diwali, the fourth day, is Balipratipada. Bali, an arrogant king in northern India, was killed by Hindu god Vishnu. The festival celebrates his downfall. Bhai Beej, the final day of the festival, symbolizes society's respect for women.

Gandhi

The Father of the Nation

Born in Porbandar, Gujarat, on October 2, 1869, Mohandas Karamchand Gandhi played a vital role in India's independence from the British. Indians know him simply as Gandhi, or the Mahatma (Great Soul).

Gandhi married Kasturba Makanji at the age of thirteen, then went to London to study law. Finishing his degree in 1891, he returned home to look for work. After unsuccessful attempts, he went to South Africa for the same reason. He was shocked by the racial discrimination there and decided to fight for the rights of Indians. In 1915, Gandhi returned to India and led nonviolent protests and resistance movements against the British colonizers. In 1919, he went into politics, and a few years later, he became head of the Indian National Congress. His methods of protest included strikes, fasting, breaking civil laws, and holding prayer meetings.

THE SUCCESSFUL MARCH

In 1930, Gandhi led a march to the sea to protest against the tax on salt. He encouraged people to make their own salt instead, which was illegal. By the following spring, making salt for personal use was permitted.

Below: Gandhi *(center)* was jailed several times by the British for his freedom protests. The British finally gave in to his demands in 1947.

Left: Gandhi spun his own simple clothes and wore them wherever he went, even to formal meetings with the British leaders.

A Dream Realized but Not Quite

In 1932, Gandhi fasted to protest the British decision to segregate the lowest caste, or the untouchables. The British reversed their decision soon after. Gandhi then embarked on a campaign to eliminate discrimination against the untouchables, whom he called *Harijans* (HUH-ri-jahn), or "children of God."

Gandhi campaigned for an independent India where Hindus and Muslims would live together in harmony. His wish, however, did not materialize. In 1947, an independent secular India and a Muslim Pakistan were created. One of the greatest disappointments for Gandhi was that the freedom of India came at the expense of Indian unity. Muslims blamed him for favoring his own people, while Hindu extremists blamed him for partitioning the country and for the violence that followed. On January 30, 1948, a Hindu fanatic opposed to Gandhi's tolerance of the Muslims shot and killed him.

Gandhi's philosophy of nonviolent protest influenced people in other parts of the world, including Dr. Martin Luther King, Jr. in his civil rights campaign in the United States and Nelson Mandela in his antiapartheid movement in South Africa.

THE GANDHI WAY

Gandhi believed there were three possible responses to oppression and injustice. One was the coward's way — to tolerate or run away from it. The second, better than the first, was to fight it by force. The third way was the one that required the most courage — to fight against oppression by nonviolent means. Gandhi insisted that nonviolent resistance should not be directed against a person, just against an unfair act.

Hindu Deities

Creator, Preserver, and Destroyer

In Hinduism, Brahman is the one great god who takes on different forms depending on his function. The Holy Trinity — the three main forms of Brahman — consists of Brahma, Vishnu, and Shiva. Brahma, the creator, has four heads facing the four directions. Vishnu, the preserver, maintains *dharma* (DHAR-mah), or law and order in the universe. Shiva, the destroyer, despite his frightening looks, is a benevolent god. According to legend, the Ganges River flowed only in heaven until it was brought down to Earth to purify our planet. It came cascading down to Earth and would have shattered Earth had not Shiva broken its fall by allowing it to fall first on his head.

Krishna: Cowherd, Lover, Hero, and God

Krishna is an incarnation of Vishnu. His mother, Devaki, was the sister of Kamsa, a wicked king. When told he would die at the hands of his sister's child, Kamsa killed all of Devaki's children, except Krishna, who was smuggled across the Yamuna River to a town. There, a cowherd raised him.

Below: Krishna is worshiped not only by Hindus in India and Asia. The Hare Krishna cult, popular in the West, evolved out of a worship of him.

Krishna, raised as a cowherd, was mischievous and played pranks on people. He also slew demons and performed miracles. He was a sought after lover among the *gopis* (GO-pees) — wives and daughters of the cowherds. The sound of his flute so mesmerized them that they left whatever they were doing to dance around him. The *Mahabharata*, which recounts the epic fight between the Pandavas and Kauravas, portrays Krishna as a hero who helps the Pandavas regain their kingdom.

The Elephant God

Ganesha, or Ganapati, is the son of Shiva and Parvati. Legend has it that Parvati formed him from the "rubbings" of her body so that he could stand guard at the door while she bathed. When Shiva came home, not knowing who the boy was and angry at being kept away from his wife, he sent his men to cut off the boy's head. When Parvati discovered this later, she was devastated. To ease his wife's grief, Shiva promised to cut off the head of the first living creature he came across and attach it to the boy's body. The creature happened to be an elephant.

MIRACLE OR MYTH?

In 1995, Hindus all over the world were intrigued by a strange happening. Ganesha statues at all temples, when offered a spoon of milk, drank from it. Some Hindus saw this as Ganesha's attempts to absolve the sins of his worshipers. Thousands flocked to the temples to "feed" him. Others remained unconvinced and gave scientific explanations for the phenomenon.

Indian Textiles

Cloth has been woven in India as far back as the Harappan civilization in the fourth century B.C. Since then, textiles have evolved as an art form, where the weaver is both a craftsperson and an artist.

Ring Shawl and Shadow Embroidery

India produces some of the world's most beautiful fabrics. One of the choicest is the "ring shawl" of Kashmir. Woven from the soft

fleece of the Himalayan ibex, a wild mountain goat, the shawl is so fine it can be pulled through a ring worn on the finger. The specialty of Lucknow is "shadow embroidery" — a herringbone stitch done on the reverse side of thin cloth.

Girls learn how to sew and embroider from an early age. They help their mothers make skirts, sarongs, turbans, scarves, and quilts, sometimes from leftover scraps of cloth. From colored threads and hundreds of mirrors, they create designs of birds and other animals, flowers, and geometric shapes.

Above: **In Rajasthan, village women's blouses and skirts twinkle with tiny mirrors embedded in brightly colored embroidery. To complement the garments, they wear heavy silver jewelry and have small flowers tattooed on their faces.**

Ikat: An Ancient Craft

Sixth-century frescoes in the Ajanta Caves depict the art of making *ikat* (IH-CUT), a term derived from a Malay-Indonesian word. Ikat fabrics, among the most highly prized textiles in the world, are made by tying sections of bundled yarn, either cotton or silk, then dying them so the exposed part gets dyed and the tied section retains its original color. The yarn is then woven into fabric, usually with geometric and floral motifs.

The most complex type of ikat, double ikat, exists today in India, where it is known as *patolu* (puh-TOH-loo). In the old days, patolu was used as coverings for royal elephants, as hangings in temples, and as shrouds for the dead before cremation. Today, the old craft of patolu survives only in Patan, Gujarat, where just two families from the ancestral patola weavers' clan practice it. Gujarat, Andhra Pradesh, and Orissa produce simpler ikat styles. The *phulkari* (puhl-KAH-ree) of the Punjab, the patchwork embroidery of Bengal, the brocaded saris of Varanasi, the heavy silks of Kanchipuram, the block-printed fabrics of Rajasthan, and the hand-painted fabrics of Gujarat and Andhra Pradesh are other well-known textiles.

Above: **A patolu sari. Many women like to wear these saris.**

Left: **A woman dries saris after dyeing them by the river bank.**

Jammu and Kashmir

Hindu and Muslim Disagreement

According to legend, an ascetic named Kashyap reclaimed some land from a vast lake in the western Himalayas and called it Kashyapamar. Various Hindu dynasties ruled this land, later named Kashmir, until 1346 when it came under Muslim rule. In 1819, the Sikh kingdom of the Punjab annexed Kashmir. Then in 1846, the Dogra (Hindu) kingdom of Jammu annexed Kashmir. When Indian independence created a Muslim Pakistan and a Hindu-dominated India, the Maharaja of Kashmir decided to join the Indian Union. Pakistan, however, contested, and because of the large number of Muslims in Kashmir, claimed the area.

Scenic Vale of Kashmir and Barren Ladakh

More than 90 percent of Jammu and Kashmir is mountainous. The state contains the Karakoram range of the Himalayas, where

Opposite: **India and Pakistan fought three inconclusive wars over Kashmir. Pakistan rules one part of the state, and India rules the other. China also claims part of Kashmir. Since the Sino-Indian war of 1962, China has been in control of northeastern Kashmir. In Jammu and Kashmir today, there is a strong Indian military presence to confront the Pakistani and Chinese forces along the borders.**

Left: **Some houses in the capital of Kashmir, Srinagar, which is in the Vale of Kashmir controlled by India.**

at least thirty peaks exceed 24,000 feet (7,315 m). The Indian part of the state has the picturesque Vale of Kashmir, which is actually an ancient lake basin at an elevation of 5,300 feet (1,615 m).

The barren landscape of Ladakh in eastern Kashmir is a stark contrast to the Vale of Kashmir. The entire area, apart from the occasional valley or water course, is hot, with straggly vegetation and limited or no rainfall. India and Pakistan contested Ladakh, and in 1949, the southern part went to India and the rest to Pakistan. In the early 1960s, Chinese forces occupied the northeastern part of the Indian portion, so now the area is divided among three countries.

The Standoff Continues

The "Kashmir problem" — whether the state should belong to India or Pakistan or, if divided, which parts should remain in either country — has been an unresolved issue since the partition of India in 1947. Pakistan has a thinly populated and underdeveloped territory, while India has the Vale of Kashmir, with a large Muslim population. Several violent separatist movements in the territory seek independence from both India and Pakistan, as a result of which tourism — one of the largest money-earners for the state — is hard hit.

HOUSEBOATS

Kashmir has several lakes. Dal Lake is the best known. Slim gondola-like boats carry passengers across the lake and to and from the houseboats moored on it. Houseboats were the British answer to a Dogra ruler's order that no non-Kashmiri could buy land or buildings in the state. The British houseboats were small, with a living/ dining room and bedroom, and they could be towed downriver to Wular Lake for the fishing season. Today, houseboats are much larger and are mostly used as hotels moored along the fringes of the Dal and Nagin lakes.

Kabaddi

Not much is known about the origin of the Indian game of kabaddi, but it is estimated to be about four thousand years old. Kabaddi was originally intended to develop quick reflexes for self defense, but it soon evolved into a team sport. It is also popular in Nepal, Bangladesh, Japan, Pakistan, and Sri Lanka.

Kabaddi is played on a 41-foot x 33-foot (12.5-m x 10-m) area, which is divided into two halves. There are two teams of twelve players. Seven play at a time, while five are in reserve. One team sends a "raider" into the opponent's court with the aim of touching as many players as he can before returning to his court. All the while, he has to chant "kabaddi-kabaddi" without drawing a breath. Whoever he touches leaves the court. The opposing team tries to avoid being touched and to hold off the raider and keep him in its court until he draws a breath, in which case he is out. The raider is also declared out if any part of his body touches the ground outside the boundary line. The teams alternate in sending raiders into each other's courts.

Below: **People of all ages enjoy watching kabaddi matches and cheering for their favorite teams. Many Indians grew up playing the game.**

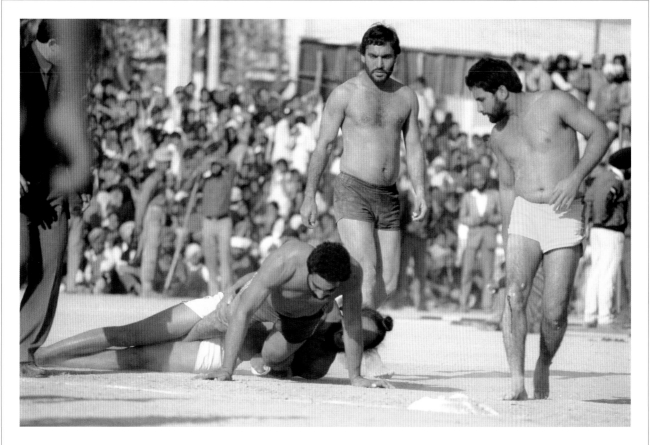

One Game but Many Forms and Names

In India, there are three forms of kabaddi: *surjeevani* (soor-JEE-vanee), *gaminee* (GAH-mi-NEE), and *amar* (UH-muhr). In surjeevani kabaddi, when one player is out, another comes in to take his place. In gaminee kabaddi, when all the players of a team are out, the game ends, so this form of kabaddi has no time limit. In amar kabaddi, when a player is touched he does not go out of the court but the raider's team gets a point. In this type of kabaddi, the time limit of the game is set in advance.

Kabaddi has a different name depending on where it is played. In the south, it is called *chedugudu* or *hu-tu-tu*. In the east, it is called *hadudu* (men) or *chu-kit-kit* (women). The Kabaddi Federation of India, which was founded in 1950, determines the duration of the game, the number of players, and other rules. The federation has also compiled rules for playing the game. Kabaddi was played as a demonstration sport at the 1936 Olympics in Berlin. In 1994, the sport was included in the Asian Games at Hiroshima. Indians hope that someday it will become an Olympic sport.

Above: "Gotcha!" A kabaddi match, which traditionally consists of two 20-minute sessions with a 5-minute break, is supervised by seven people — a referee, two linesmen, two umpires, a scorer, and a timekeeper. Because the game is simple and requires no equipment, it is popular in rural India.

Nehru-Gandhi Dynasty

Born in 1889, Jawaharlal Nehru went to school in England when he was fifteen, and later to Trinity College, Cambridge, where he got a degree in natural science. He also studied law. In 1912, he returned to India to join his father's legal practice and attended a meeting of the Congress Party.

At twenty-six, Nehru married Kamala Kaul, with whom he had a daughter, Indira. He then decided to give up law and devote himself fully to politics. In 1921, both Nehru and his father were arrested for protesting the festivities that honored Prince Edward's visit to India. In 1929 and again in 1936, Nehru served as president of the Indian National Congress. When India gained independence on August 15, 1947, Nehru became the first prime minister of the country.

Tragedy Strikes the Gandhis

In 1942, Indira married Feroze Gandhi and had two sons, Rajiv and Sanjay. She later left her husband's house and moved into her father's official residence with her children. After Nehru's death in 1964, Lal Bahadur Shastri became prime minister, and Indira became minister of information and broadcasting in his government. When Shastri died in 1966, Indira was nominated as a candidate to succeed him. She won the election.

In 1975, the courts ruled against Indira for electoral malpractice, which meant she would lose her seat in parliament, so she declared a state of emergency in the country and imprisoned her political opponents. She called for elections in 1977. A coalition of parties formed the Janata government and defeated Indira and her party. The Janata government, however, could not sustain itself for long and soon dissolved. In the 1980 elections, Indira won a seat.

On June 23, 1980, Indira's son Sanjay Gandhi, her politically active son, was killed in a flying accident. Indira then summoned Rajiv Gandhi, a pilot, to take Sanjay's place in politics. In 1984, Indira was assassinated by her bodyguards. Rajiv was sworn in as her successor. He called for elections soon after and won. He remained prime minister until 1989. In 1991, while campaigning for election, he was killed by a suicide bomber.

Above: **Jawaharlal Nehru was independent India's first prime minister. In 1937, his sister Vijaya Lakshmi became India's first woman minister in the United Provinces (now Uttar Pradesh). In 1953, she became the president of the United Nations General Assembly — the first woman ever to hold this position.**

Opposite: **In 1984, Indira Gandhi (shown here with her supporters) carried out Operation Bluestar against Jarnail Singh Bhindranwale, a Sikh fundamentalist who barricaded himself and his followers in the Golden Temple in Amritsar. The Indian Army stormed the temple and killed Bhindranwale and his followers. A few months later, Indira's Sikh bodyguards assassinated her at her residence.**

63

Overpopulation

India, with a population of almost a billion, is the second most populous nation in the world after China. The capital, New Delhi, is home to 9.2 million people. It is predicted that by the year 2050, India will be the most populous country in the world. Given that the land area of India is only one-third that of the United States, overpopulation is a serious strain on the country's resources.

The Whys and Wherefores

Although child marriage is banned, people, especially in rural areas, tend to marry young, which means longer childbearing

years that, in turn, mean more children. The uneducated are generally ignorant about the benefits of small families and are reluctant to learn family planning techniques. Another reason for the population increase is the influx of refugees and illegal immigrants into India. In 1947, when the country was divided into a Muslim Pakistan and a secular India, many Muslims in India migrated to Pakistan, but the entire Hindu and Sikh populations of East and West Pakistan came to India.

In 1971, when East Pakistan struggled to break free from West Pakistan to form Bangladesh, refugees again came to India. A fresh exodus of minority Hindus arrived in India when

Above: **Rush hour traffic at Churchgate Station, Mumbai, gives a clue as to the number of people in India.**

Left: Major cities have shantytowns, with "houses" made of cardboard and corrugated iron or polyethylene sheets, where locals as well as immigrants live in cramped conditions. Because one-third of India's population lives in extreme poverty, children are often seen not as mouths to be fed but as a means to increase the family income. Some children are put to work from the young ages of eight to ten years. They plow fields, sew garments, sell wares, and basically do anything to bring in more money for the family.

Bangladesh declared itself a Muslim republic. The creation of Bangladesh also caused panic among its non-Bengali residents, who subsequently settled in India. The country also attracts illegal immigrants seeking employment opportunities. Among them are large numbers of Bangladeshis in Assam and Bengal and Nepalis all over northern and eastern India.

Measures to Stop the Population Explosion

Despite an increase in economic productivity, as well as major advances in agricultural and industrial development, India compares poorly with other developing nations in some areas. Unemployment, for instance, is on the increase. International aid has helped India a little. Foreign aid for birth control began in 1966. The same year, the United States, Sweden, and other international organizations gave hundreds of millions of rupees in aid to India. In recent years, the World Bank has asked India to popularize the use of male contraceptive methods.

Below: A family planning poster in India appeals for a stop to the growing population.

For every 100 persons in the world today, over 15 live in India.

You can help.

Project Tiger

Tiger, Tiger, Burning Out

At the turn of the twentieth century, about forty thousand tigers roamed the forests of India. By 1969, only about three thousand were left. In 1940, Jim Corbett, a British hunter in India, wanted to regulate the hunting of tigers and the felling of forests. He felt that if these measures were not enforced, the population of tigers would not last beyond the twentieth century.

Indiscriminate killing took place in the first half of the century. The Maharaja of Udaipur shot at least 1,000 tigers. In 1921, British General Wardrop shot seven adult tigers within a

week. Despite Corbett's warnings, the British and the maharajas of India continued killing the animal for sport.

A 1972 census revealed that there were only about two thousand tigers in India, six to seven hundred in Myanmar, and another six to seven hundred in Bangladesh, Nepal, and Bhutan. Guy Mountfort, a conservationist, proposed an international effort to create reserves for the tiger. Indira Gandhi, then prime minister of India, showed a strong interest in wildlife conservation, and, in 1972, Project Tiger was launched at the Corbett National Park in Uttar Pradesh.

Above and *opposite:* **A major predator has now become the prey. Because the tiger represents great strength, some people believe that all parts of its body — bones, claws, teeth, etc. — ward off evil and give courage. Poachers, thus, kill tigers for the value of their body parts.**

The hunting of tigers was strictly controlled by the Convention on International Trade in Endangered Species (CITES). The import and export of tiger skins and parts were also banned. Tigers were given legal protection, and fifteen protected and well-managed reserves were created for them: Corbett National Park, Dudhwa, Indravati, Jaldapara, Kanha, Manas, Melghat, Mudumalai, Nagarjunasagar, Palamau, Periyar, Ranthambhor, Sariska, the Sundarbans, and Wayanaad.

Problems in the Early Stages of the Project

Initially, the project encountered problems. Villagers were relocated from their homes to create the reserves. Tour operators felt the reserves would threaten their livelihood. Serious

VALMIK THAPAR

A leading tiger expert named Valmik Thapar is urging countries, such as Japan, to stop the illegal trade of tiger parts. He feels that trade in tiger parts represents a breakdown in Indian tradition in which tigers played a significant role. Although some Indian forest communities keep shrines to the tiger, this tribal culture is giving way to Western influences.

opposition arose in the early 1980s when tigers killed a number of villagers. Pressure was put on the government to allow hunting again. The killings, however, occurred because the villagers had encroached into the buffer zone around the reserves to cultivate crops, and the tigers attacked them. The villagers, realizing their mistake, decided to keep their distance from the buffer zone, and the incidence of attacks decreased.

Poaching is still a serious threat to the tiger population, especially with the large market for tiger skins and body parts in some parts of Asia.

Sikhism

Guru Nanak (1469–1539) founded Sikhism, a religion that combines Islam and Hinduism, in the late fifteenth century. His beliefs are detailed in the holy book *Guru Granth Sahib*. Sikhs regard themselves as disciples of Guru Nanak and his nine successors. In Sikhism, God is not represented by idols. Followers serve God with prayers and a life of obedience to His commands.

The Nine Successors

The second guru was Guru Angad (1504–1552). He popularized the Gurmukhi script, introduced by Guru Nanak, and encouraged his followers to read religious literature. He also introduced the *langar* (LAN-gar), a free meal where everyone sits down together and eats the same food.

Guru Amardas (1479–1574) focused on the spread of Sikhism. Guru Ramdas, the fourth guru, established the town of Ramdaspur, which developed into the city of Amritsar. Guru Arjun (1563–1606) built the Harimandir (Temple of God), or Golden Temple. He also compiled the writings of the earlier gurus into the *Guru Granth Sahib*, now housed in the Golden Temple.

FIGHTING FOR THEIR OWN HOME

The Sikhs in India are fighting with the Indian government for a separate homeland. Unfortunately, they have turned to violence to achieve their goal. In 1984, they assassinated Indira Gandhi, then prime minister of India, after which Hindus rioted and killed hundreds of Sikhs.

Opposite: Poster of Guru Nanak and his nine successors. Together, they are the ten gurus of Sikhism.

Below: The Golden Temple, the holiest Sikh shrine at Amritsar, is situated in the middle of a lake.

The Mughal king, Jahangir, became jealous of Guru Arjun's influence, since even Muslims were going to the Harimandir to pray. He asked Guru Arjun to change the text in the *Guru Granth Sahib* to include praises of Prophet Muhammad. When Guru Arjun refused, he was tortured to death. Guru Arjun thus became the first martyr in Sikh history. Guru Har Gobind (1595–1644), Guru Arjun's successor, formed an army to guard against Mughal tyranny.

Guru Har Rai (1630–1661) urged his followers to meditate and lead a life of self-discipline. Guru Harkrishan (1656-1664) became a guru at the age of five and is a favorite among children. Guru Tegh Bahadur (1621–1675), who succeeded him, sacrificed his life protecting Hindus from the Mughal king Aurangzeb, who forced Hindus under his rule to convert to Islam. Guru Tegh Bahadur thus became the second Sikh martyr.

Guru Tegh Bahadur's son, Guru Gobind Singh (1666–1708), became the tenth guru. He founded the Khalsa fraternity, which is the main Sikh order today. Its members take "Singh" (meaning lion) or "Kaur" (meaning lioness) as their middle name. Guru Gobind Singh declared *Guru Granth Sahib* the last guru. In other words, Sikhs were to worship the book as if it were a guru.

SIKHS OUTSIDE INDIA

Sikhs are concentrated in four main areas outside India: Canada, the United States, Great Britain, and the Far East. In 1969, Sardar Harbhajan Singh Puri emigrated from Delhi to Canada, and then to the United States. He began teaching yoga classes in Los Angeles and gathered a number of American students, to whom he gradually introduced a form of Sikhism. His movement, called 3HO (Healthy, Happy, Holy Organization), spread to various parts of the United States.

Taj Mahal

Wonder of the World

The Taj Mahal is located on the southern bank of the Yamuna River just outside Agra. The palace epitomizes Mughal emperor Shah Jahan's love for his wife, Mumtaz Mahal. After her sudden death in 1631 while giving birth to their fourteenth child, the emperor decided to build a unique mausoleum in her honor.

Construction of the Taj Mahal began in 1632. A council of architects, including people from India, Persia, and Central Asia, submitted their plans to the emperor. A great patron of architecture, Shah Jahan took a personal interest in the designs, modifying them as he saw fit.

The mausoleum was completed in 1643, and the first memorial service for Mumtaz Mahal was held in it the same year. The immediate adjuncts of the palace were completed in 1649. The entire complex was carefully planned and built, because an Islamic law dictates that once a tomb is completed, nothing can be added to or taken away from it. When Aurangzeb, Shah Jahan's son, imprisoned him at the nearby Agra Fort, Shah Jahan spent his last years (1658–1666) gazing longingly at the Taj Mahal.

Above: Shah Jahan, the Mughal emperor who built the Taj Mahal, reigned from 1628 to 1658.

Left: The Taj Mahal is made of pure white marble. Adjacent buildings are made of red sandstone from local quarries. Forty-three kinds of gems, from Turkestan in Central Asia, Tibet, Upper Burma, Badakshan in Afghanistan, Egypt, and other places, embellished the interior and exterior of the mausoleum.

Inside, the Taj Mahal is divided into five chambers. In an octagonal burial chamber, there are two marble tombs. An octagonal, filigreed marble screen surrounds the two tombs. Rare stones adorn the tombs, and they are further beautified by fine mosaics and calligraphy. Passages from the Quran are inscribed on the interior and exterior of the Taj Mahal.

At his death in 1666, Shah Jahan was buried beside Mumtaz Mahal. The bodies are not in the tombs but in a small crypt below the burial chamber. Legend has it that Shah Jahan planned to construct a black replica of the Taj Mahal across the river from Mumtaz Mahal's tomb for himself.

Below: **More than twenty thousand workers labored daily on the Taj Mahal. The entire complex took twenty-two years to complete.**

Standing Tall through the Passage of Time

The Taj Mahal has long been regarded as the pinnacle of Mughal architecture. Humayun's tomb in Delhi, with its white marble dome and an inner octagonal burial chamber, is considered an important precursor of the Taj Mahal. With the decline of the Mughal Empire in the eighteenth century, the Taj Mahal suffered some severe setbacks. Over the years, many of the gems inlaid in its walls were stolen. Under the British Raj, plans were made to demolish the Taj Mahal and sell the marble in England. The plan fell through due to a lack of prospective buyers.

DAMAGE CONTROL

The Taj Mahal's white marble is turning yellow with age, pollution, and sharp changes in temperature. Some steps taken to remedy the situation include replacing cracked or dirty slabs and applying a special mixture over the marble to absorb dust and other chemicals.

Tea

According to an Indian legend, a sage once vowed to meditate without closing his eyes, but he failed. Upset, he tore off his eyelids and flung them to the ground. Soon, each eyelash grew into a plant. By boiling the leaves of the plant in water, a person could stay awake. This legend was said to be the origin of the first tea plant in India.

In 1850, British Lieutenant Robert Bruce found tea growing wild in the forests of Assam. Soon after, the East India Company set up the first commercial tea plantation. For almost half a century, the British monopolized the tea industry.

A Money Spinner

Tea is now cultivated in West Bengal, Assam, and Tripura in the northeast, Kerala and Tamil Nadu in the south, and Himachal Pradesh in the north. India's annual production amounts to over 1.5 million pounds (700 million kilograms). Tea is one of India's largest foreign exchange earners. The industry employs over two million workers.

Below: Tea plantations are carpets of green that follow the contours of the land as far as the eye can see. The tea plant, if allowed to grow to its full size, reaches a height of 25 to 30 feet (7 to 9 m). Since only its leaves are harvested, the plant is pruned down for easy plucking.

Left: Tea leaves — ideally two open leaves and a bud — are plucked off the bushes at weekly intervals during the February/ March to November season. Because the tea leaf bruises easily, it must be handled gently. For this reason, plucking is done mostly by women.

A Tea to Suit Your Taste

Orthodox tea, one of the varieties of black tea, has a strong aroma but is not strong tasting. After harvesting, the leaf is allowed to dry for sixteen to eighteen hours so it becomes soft. It is then rolled in rolling machines, fermented, and dried in drying machines at carefully controlled temperatures. The tea is then sorted by size into different grades.

Green tea is popular in Afghanistan, Kashmir, Japan, and a few other countries. Although made like orthodox tea, the leaves are not fermented. Immediately after harvesting, the leaves are put into vats of boiling water to kill the enzymes that cause fermentation. Then they are rolled and dried. Green tea looks similar to orthodox tea but has a faint greenish tinge.

Most of the tea in India is produced by the CTC (cut, tear, curl) process, where the tea leaves, instead of being rolled, are fed into machines for processing. There are no whole leaves in the finished tea. India is the only country that manufactures and exports both orthodox and CTC tea.

RECIPE FOR MASALA TEA

Pour a cup of milk and a cup of water into a pot. Add a quarter teaspoon of crushed ginger, one split pod of cardamom, and sugar to taste. Heat the mixture over medium heat. When it boils, turn off the heat and add two teaspoons of tea leaves. Cover the pot and let the leaves steep in the hot liquid for a minute. Strain. Indians believe this tea cures coughs and colds.

RELATIONS WITH NORTH AMERICA

India and the United States are the two largest democracies in the world, and both countries look upon individual freedom as an important ideal. The two countries are multiracial and multiethnic societies in which all citizens are free to practice their own religion and customs. Their constitutions, too, show similarities. They share the concept of a society based on equality for all, irrespective of religious or ethnic background.

When Christopher Columbus sailed west from Spain and landed in North America in the late fifteenth century, he thought he had reached India and so named the natives Indians. This mistake continues to create linguistic confusion, with people

Opposite: **The Hare Krishna movement, formally known as the International Society for Krishna Consciousness, has its main office in Los Angeles. It was founded by an Indian ascetic, A. C. Bhaktivedanta, in 1966. Since then, the movement has gained momentum in India and abroad.**

having to distinguish themselves as American Indians, West Indians, and East or Asian Indians.

In the eighteenth century, trade between the United States and India led to the establishment of a U.S. consulate in Calcutta. Because India was not an independent nation, it had no political interaction with other countries. The U.S. government conducted business with India through the British embassy in Washington, D.C. Britain did not encourage direct trade between the two countries. Today, the United States is India's chief trading partner.

Above: **For Indians who can afford it, especially the young, wearing U.S. fashion labels is a must.**

Calling Another Land Their Home

In the late nineteenth and early twentieth century, it was not easy for Indians to go to the United States. Few had the means or the courage to leave their homeland and deal with an alien culture.

In 1898, a few revolutionaries working for India's independence went to the United States and lived as exiles. Some Americans — Mary Das, Agnes Smedley, W. A. and Marion Wotherspoon, Moorfield Storey, and Robert Morss Lovett, among others — helped them in their efforts.

Between 1898 and 1902, a severe drought in the Punjab led to a sizeable number of Sikhs emigrating to the United States and Canada. In the period 1900–1910 alone, about five thousand Sikhs arrived in the Pacific Northwest. Experienced farmers, many found employment as laborers in California's Sacramento and San Joaquin valleys, as well as in the fig orchards and vineyards near Fresno.

Western Pacific hired a number of Sikhs to build railroads; other Sikhs found employment in the lumber mills of Washington State. One well-documented labor group, led by Tuly Singh Johl, helped build the Marysville railway station in California. More Sikhs emigrated after this. Soon, the large Sikh groups built gurdwaras in Stockton and El Centro, with kitchens and dormitories to cater to travelers and the sick.

In 1913, Har Dayal, who came to the United States to study Buddhism at Harvard University, organized the Ghadar Party (*ghadar* means "revolt" in Urdu) to garner support for India's independence from British rule. When officials foiled his attempts, many of the Party's leaders were disillusioned and returned to India.

Barring Entry

The U.S. Congress passed the Barred Zone Act in 1917, prohibiting immigration from a number of countries, including India. Because of the new immigration law, Indians who had legally emigrated to the United States earlier found that their wives and children could not join them. After 1917, the U.S. government denaturalized some Indians. In spite of the Barred Zone Act, between 1917 and 1930, about three thousand Indian immigrants entered the country illegally. Almost no emigration from India to the United States occurred between 1931 and 1940.

Above: **Swami Vivekananda (1863–1902), a Hindu spiritual leader fluent in English, addressed the World Parliament of Religions in Chicago in 1893. He gave talks on Vedantic philosophy, explaining his ideas on the nature of the soul and human destiny. Soon, Vedanta Society centers sprang up all around the United States. Vedantic thought has influenced many American historians and philosophers.**

Opening the Doors

Until 1947, there were few Indian students in U.S. universities. After independence, however, more Indians went to the United States to study because of the scholarships offered. After graduation, many of them found jobs in the United States and stayed. Those who returned to India were disappointed that the country was not yet ready to use their talents. Students now account for one-third of Indians in the United States.

The 1950s and 1960s saw an increase in the number of Indians going to the United States. Modified laws allowed the families of U.S. citizens and permanent residents to enter. By 1976, India became the biggest source of foreign physicians in the United States. Today, 5 percent of doctors in the United States are of Indian origin.

In 1972, when Idi Amin expelled Asians from Uganda, many of them arrived as refugees to North America. Some Ugandan Indians, mostly Gujaratis, entered the motel business in Georgia, Oklahoma, California, Texas, Mississippi, and parts of Canada.

Below: **An Indian student (shown here in red) and her U.S. classmates brainstorm ideas for a project.**

Integrating Into a New Society

The first Indian immigrants came to Canada between 1905 and 1908. They were mostly Sikhs. The immigrants found work as unskilled laborers in railroad construction and in the logging and lumber industries in Vancouver and British Columbia. Facing considerable hostility and racial discrimination there, many of them moved to northern Washington, Oregon, and California in the United States.

After 1908, a government order stopped the migration of Indians to Canada. Because some of them were actively involved in driving the British out of India, there were already anti-Asian sentiments in Quebec, Saskatchewan, and Nova Scotia. Shunned by the white majority, the Indians built their own community structures.

Indians who migrated to Canada after 1947 have been better able to integrate into Canadian society. According to the 1991 census, 3 percent of the Indians living in Canada arrived before 1961, 15 percent arrived in the 1960s, and over 80 percent arrived in the 1970s and 1980s.

Above: Indians, especially those born in the United States and Canada, have integrated well into their respective societies. Children born in North America of Indian descent attend school and take part in extracurricular activities. Indian-born parents, however, are a little apprehensive about the influence of North American mainstream culture on their children. The Sikhs have been the most successful group in retaining their Indian culture. Almost all second-generation Sikh Americans and Canadians, for example, understand Punjabi.

Holding Their Own

Many of the families of early immigrants have their own businesses, such as hotels. Indians own 30 percent of all the hotels and motels in the United States. Most Indians in the United States are well educated and hold professional jobs. Many Indian men hold managerial, professional, or technical jobs, and more than half of them have college degrees. These levels are the highest for any ethnic group in the United States. An Indian family's median income is higher than most other U.S. households.

In the 1970s and 1980s, the U.S. computer industry was fast expanding. Indians flocked to the United States eager to participate in the development of new technology. Many Indian companies are now working with U.S. manufacturers.

Medicine is another field where Indians have a large presence. One in twenty physicians in the United States today obtained his or her primary medical degree in India. In 1995, a seventeen-year-old Indian named Balamurali Ambati became the world's youngest doctor when he received his degree from Mount Sinai School of Medicine in New York — he broke the record set by an eighteen-year-old Israeli medical student.

NOT TO BE OUTDONE

Forty-five percent of Indian women in the United States are employed outside the home. One-third of Indian-American doctors in the United States are women. Among second-generation Indian-Americans, the occupational distribution between the sexes is nearly equal.

Below: India is the third largest source of software engineers in the world, after the United States and France.

Trade with Canada

Trade relations between India and Canada began only after 1947. Today, the two countries share a significant amount of trade. Nuclear cooperation between them, however, was suspended following India's first nuclear test in 1974.

Canada has traditionally supplied India with raw materials and semi-finished products, such as potash, pulp and paper, steel, aluminum, and zinc. Indian exports to Canada include tea, coffee, textiles, carpets, and footwear. With the liberalization of India's economy, joint Indo-Canadian ventures in power generation, telecommunications, electronics, plastics, mining, automobile components, food processing, and pharmaceuticals have either been formed or are in the planning stages.

Since 1982, the Canada India Business Council has been organizing trade missions to India and has signed a joint protocol with the Federation of Indian Chambers of Commerce and Industry — the largest Indian business organization. Trade relations between the two countries are governed by the General Agreement on Tariffs and Trade (GATT). India is given special status so that its imports are subject to lower tariffs.

Opposite: **Bangalore, or the "Silicon Valley of India," has a large population of well-educated, high-income young people in the software industry. The city has domestic firms and a healthy mix of foreign ones, such as IBM, Motorola, and Texas Instruments. Bangalore also has a cyber café, where people can sip a cup of coffee while surfing the Internet.**

Below: **Canada imports carpets such as these from India. The quality of carpets depends on the intricacy and beauty of the design, as well as the density and skill of the knotting.**

Trade with the United States

At the time of independence, India had significant trade with the United States, but trade declined when India aligned itself with the Soviet Union. In 1991, when the Indian government liberalized its economy, U.S. investment increased.

In 1990, the United States accounted for 15 percent of India's exports. In the first six months of 1997, its exports to India increased 21 percent to total $1.8 billion. Today, Levi Strauss, Nike, and other well-known U.S. consumer goods companies have set up shop in India. When the first Levis store opened in Bangalore, almost all the jeans were snapped up immediately.

The U.S.-India Trade Mission in December 1997 was held to promote trade opportunities between the two countries, as well as to support the efforts of the U.S.-India Commercial Alliance and U.S.-India Business Council. The same month, the first-ever web site for a U.S. trade mission was launched. A collaborative effort between the U.S. Department of Commerce, the Confederation of Indian Industry, and TradeAccess, the web site allows U.S. and Indian businesses to interact with one another.

SANCTIONS FOR NUCLEAR TESTS

On May 11, 1998, India conducted three successful underground nuclear tests. Many countries condemned these tests, and the United States warned India of possible sanctions. When India conducted two more nuclear tests two days later, the Clinton Administration imposed sanctions that could cost India up to $20 billion in U.S. and international loans.

Influences Go Both Ways

American life has influenced the practice of Hinduism in the United States. For example, some young Hindus eat beef, a taboo in Hindu society. Hinduism has affected American life as well, through ayurveda, yoga, and transcendental meditation. Ayurveda, a traditional Indian system of medicine that emphasizes physical, mental, and spiritual balance, uses herbal medicine, diet, yoga, and meditation to cure illness. Dr. Deepak Chopra is a well-known proponent of meditative and ayurvedic healing, and his books on the subject are widely read. Demi Moore and several other American actors are fans of Chopra.

Indian textiles and garments are popular in North America. Batik fabrics are used as wall hangings and upholstery, and cotton garments are imported from India. Indian restaurants in most American cities serve foods ranging from the south Indian *idli* (ID-li) and dosai to the north Indian tandoori chicken and *naan* (NAHN). American food, too, has influenced the eating habits of Indians. Hamburgers and hot dogs are popular not only with Indians in the United States but also with Indians in India.

Below: **Yoga classes are popular in India and in North America.**

Fusing Two Different Types of Music

Indian music has crept into American society in a number of ways. In 1965, Ali Akbar Khan, who plays the *sarod* (suh-ROD), an Indian musical instrument that looks like a guitar, taught Hindustani vocal and instrumental music in the United States. In 1968, he founded the Ali Akbar Khan College of Music in Marin County, California, where he teaches nine months a year.

John McLaughlin, an American, was a guitarist with the Miles Davis group and later led a jazz-rock fusion group that played Indo-jazz. Shakti, one of the best-known Indo-jazz groups, featured L. Shankar on the violin; T. H. "Vikku" Vinayakram on the *ghatam* (GHAH-tum), or clay pot; Zakir Hussein on the *tabla* (tub-LAH), or Indian drum; and John McLaughlin on the guitar.

Warren Senders, an American vocalist, bassist, and composer who studied Western music performance, theory, and history, was drawn to Hindustani music from the first time he heard it. Senders, who now shuttles between Cambridge, Massachusetts, and Pune, India, specializes in *khayal* (khuh-YAHL), a vocal form of Hindustani classical music, and has a band called Antigravity.

Left: **Pandit Ravi Shankar, who for several years taught music in the department of ethnomusicology, UCLA, has given the sitar international popularity. He has influenced jazz and rock music, and has also contributed significantly to the rise of sitar-accompanied Western music called "raga rock." Beginning in the 1960s, his musical association with former Beatle George Harrison popularized his music in the West. As a recognition of Shankar's contribution to music, the 1998 Polar Music Prize, viewed as the Nobel prize for music, was awarded to him. The seventy-seven-year-old Shankar now lives in Los Angeles.**

Contributions by Indians

On November 19, 1997, Kalpana Chawla became the first Indian-born American to fly in a U.S. spacecraft. She was part of the team aboard the Space Shuttle *Columbia* Flight STS-87.

A team at Lederle Laboratories headed by Dr. Y. Subba Row (1896–1948) discovered aureomycin, an antibiotic that is an alternative treatment for infections that do not respond to penicillin and streptomycin. In 1968, Dr. Har Gobind Khorana, a professor at the Massachusetts Institute of Technology, jointly won the Nobel Prize in Physiology or Medicine with Robert W. Holley and Marshall W. Nirenberg. The Indian-born American astrophysicist Subrahmanyan Chandrasekhar won the 1983 Nobel Prize for Physics for his work on the evolution of stars. He shared the award with William A. Fowler of the United States.

IMPORTANT RESEARCH

Many Indians are presently doing important scientific research in the United States. At the Rockefeller Institute, Dr. H. L. Arora is researching the growth of optic nerve fibers and brain tissues in fish. This work has led to discoveries about the human brain, memory system, and behavior.

Carving a Niche for Themselves

Syed Hussain, who arrived in the United States in 1923, was the main exponent of Mahatma Gandhi's ideals. He lectured at the University of California on the history and civilization of India and was, until 1947, chairman of the National Committee for India's Independence in Washington, D.C.

Gobindram Watumal, who was responsible for financing India's freedom struggle and Indians' demands for citizenship, founded the Watumal Foundation, which grants scholarships to young Sindhis for study in the United States. The foundation also gives grants to U.S. universities to buy books about India. It gives biennial awards to the authors of the best books on India published in the United States.

Silicon Valley in California has its share of Indians who have made names for themselves. Samir Arora's NetObjects hit the headlines when IBM bought a majority share in it in April 1997. Vinod Dham headed the Intel Corporation teams that created the two industry-standard computer chips — the 486 microprocessor and the Pentium chip. Together, they give Intel a virtual monopoly in the computer hardware market. Dham is now working on K-6, the fastest X86 chip in the world.

Below: **The first Indian elected to serve in the U.S. House of Representatives was Dalip Singh Saund (shown here with his family). He was reelected twice, but his term ended when he fell ill in 1962.**

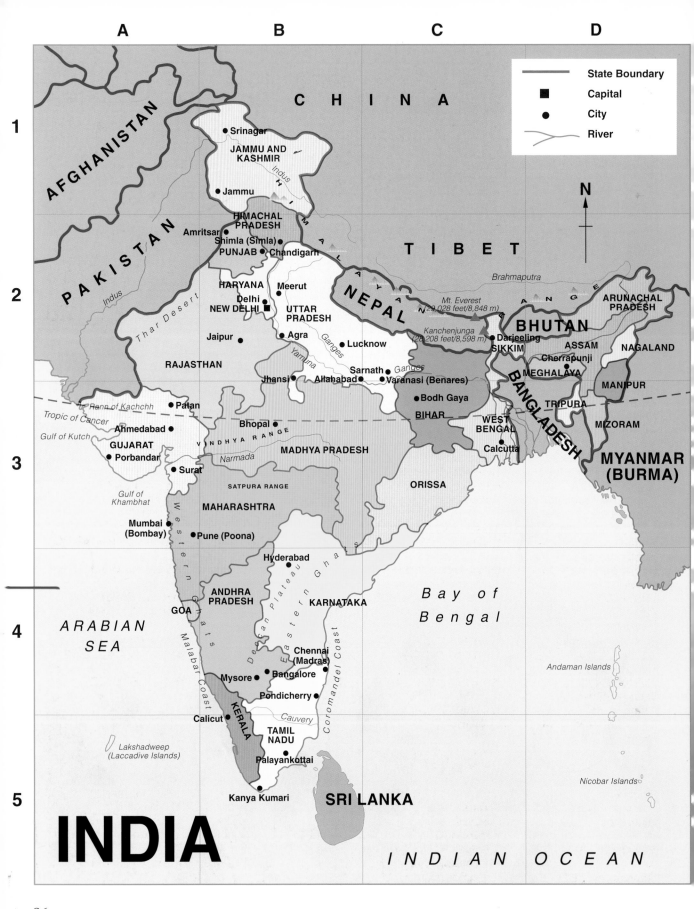

INDIA

Legend:
- State Boundary
- Capital
- City
- River

N

CHINA
AFGHANISTAN
PAKISTAN

1
• Srinagar
JAMMU AND KASHMIR
• Jammu
HIMACHAL PRADESH
Amritsar •
Shimla (Simla) •
PUNJAB • Chandigarh
Indus

2
HARYANA
• Meerut
Delhi •
NEW DELHI ■
UTTAR PRADESH
NEPAL
Brahmaputra
TIBET
Mt. Everest (29,028 feet/8,848 m)
Kanchenjunga (28,208 feet/8,598 m)
• Darjeeling
SIKKIM
BHUTAN
ARUNACHAL PRADESH
ASSAM
• Cherrapunji
NAGALAND
MEGHALAYA
MANIPUR
BANGLADESH
TRIPURA
MIZORAM
MYANMAR (BURMA)
Thar Desert
Indus
• Jaipur
RAJASTHAN
• Agra
Ganges
• Lucknow
Yamuna
Jhansi •
Sarnath •
Allahabad •
Varanasi (Benares)
Ganges
• Bodh Gaya
BIHAR
WEST BENGAL
• Calcutta

3
Rann of Kachchh
• Patan
Tropic of Cancer
Gulf of Kutch
Ahmedabad •
GUJARAT
• Porbandar
• Bhopal
VINDHYA RANGE
Narmada
MADHYA PRADESH
ORISSA
• Surat
Gulf of Khambhat
SATPURA RANGE
MAHARASHTRA
Western Ghats
Mumbai (Bombay) •
• Pune (Poona)

4
ARABIAN SEA
• Hyderabad
ANDHRA PRADESH
Deccan Plateau
KARNATAKA
Eastern Ghats
Bay of Bengal
Andaman Islands
GOA
Malabar Coast
Chennai (Madras) •
Mysore •
• Bangalore
Pondicherry •
Coromandel Coast
KERALA
Cauvery
Calicut •
Lakshadweep (Laccadive Islands)
TAMIL NADU
Nicobar Islands
• Palayankottai

5
• Kanya Kumari
SRI LANKA
INDIAN OCEAN

Above: A yogi in a meditative pose near a beach.

Afghanistan A1
Agra B2
Ahmedabad A3
Allahabad B2
Amritsar B2
Andaman Islands D4
Andhra Pradesh B4
Arabian Sea A4
Arunachal Pradesh D2
Assam D2

Bangalore B4
Bangladesh D3
Bay of Bengal C4
Bhopal B3
Bhutan D2
Bihar C3
Bodh Gaya C3
Brahmaputra River C2

Calcutta C3
Calicut B5
Cauvery River B5
Chandigarh B2
Chennai (Madras) B4
Cherrapunji D2
China B1–C1
Coromandel Coast B4

Darjeeling C2
Deccan Plateau B4
Delhi B2

Eastern Ghats B4

Ganges River B2

Goa A4
Gujarat A3
Gulf of Khambhat A3
Gulf of Kutch A3

Haryana B2
Himachal Pradesh B2
Himalayan Range B1–D2
Hyderabad B4

Indian Ocean C5–D5
Indus River A2–B2

Jaipur B2
Jammu B1
Jammu and Kashmir B1
Jhansi B2

Kanchenjunga C2
Kanya Kumari B5
Karnataka B4
Kerala B4–B5

Lakshadweep A5
Lucknow B2

Madhya Pradesh B3
Maharashtra B3
Malabar Coast A4
Manipur D3
Meerut B2
Meghalaya D2
Mizoram D3
Mt. Everest C2
Mumbai (Bombay) A3
Myanmar (Burma) D3

Mysore B4

Nagaland D2
Narmada River B3
Nepal B2
New Delhi B2
Nicobar Islands D5

Orissa C3

Pakistan A2
Palayankottai B5
Patan A3
Pondicherry B4
Porbandar A3
Pune (Poona) A3
Punjab B2

Rajasthan A2
Rann of Kachchh A3

Sarnath C2

Satpura Range B3
Shimla (Simla) B2
Sikkim C2
Sri Lanka B5
Srinagar B1
Surat A3

Tamil Nadu B5
Thar Desert A2
Tibet C2
Tripura D3
Tropic of Cancer A3–D3

Uttar Pradesh B2

Varanasi (Benares) C2
Vindhya Range B3

West Bengal C3
Western Ghats A3–B4

Yamuna River B2

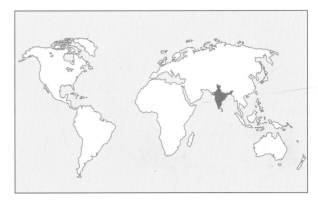

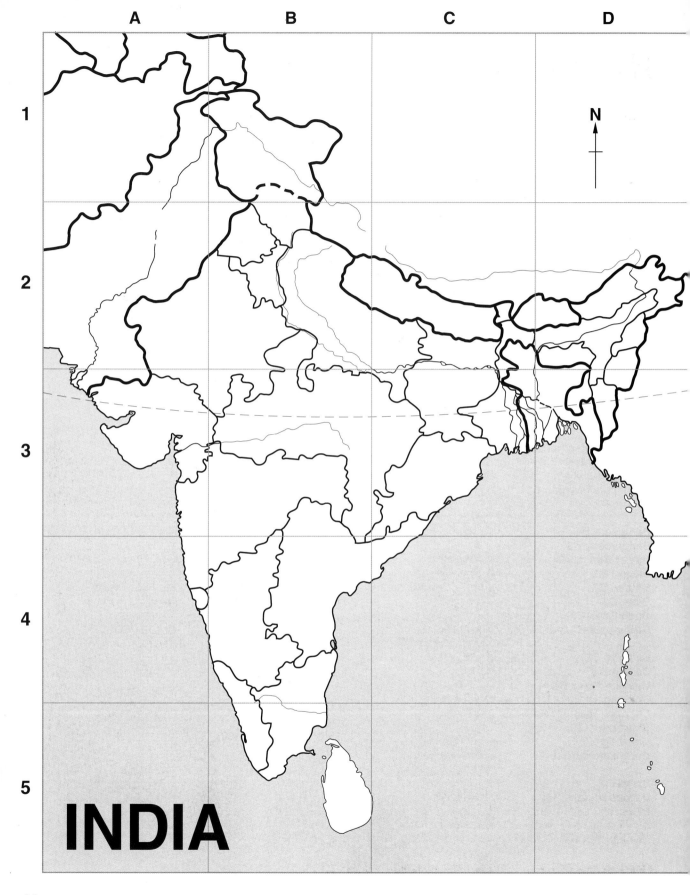

INDIA

How Is Your Geography?

Learning to identify the main geographical areas and points of a country can be challenging. Although it may seem difficult at first to memorize the location and spelling of major cities or the names of mountain ranges, rivers, deserts, lakes, and other prominent physical features, the end result of this effort can be very rewarding. Places you previously did not know existed will suddenly come to life when referred to in world news, whether in newspapers, television reports, or other books and reference sources. This knowledge will make you feel a bit closer to the rest of the world, with its fascinating variety of cultures and physical geography.

Used in a classroom setting, the instructor can make duplicates of this map using a copy machine (PLEASE DO NOT WRITE IN THIS BOOK!). Students can then fill in any requested information on their individual map copies. Used one-on-one, the student can also make copies of the map on a copy machine and use them as a study tool. The student can practice identifying place names and geographical features on his or her own.

Above: **Swamp Deer in Dudhwa National Park in Uttar Pradesh.**

India at a Glance

Land Area	1.3 million square miles (3.4 million sq km)
Population	936 million (1996/1997)
States	Andhra Pradesh, Arunachal Pradesh, Assam, Bihar, Goa, Gujarat, Haryana, Himachal Pradesh, Jammu and Kashmir, Karnataka, Kerala, Madhya Pradesh, Maharashtra, Manipur, Meghalaya, Mizoram, Nagaland, Orissa, Punjab, Rajasthan, Sikkim, Tamil Nadu, Tripura, Uttar Pradesh, and West Bengal
Union Territories	Andaman and Nicobar islands, Chandigarh, Dadra and Nagar Haveli, Daman and Diu, Lakshadweep, New Delhi, and Pondicherry
Capital	New Delhi
Important Cities	Bangalore, Calcutta, Chennai, Hyderabad, Mumbai, and New Delhi.
National Animal	Tiger
National Bird	Peacock
Highest Mountain	Kanchenjunga (28,208 feet/8,598 m)
Major Rivers	Brahmaputra
	Ganges
	Indus
Official Languages	Assamese, Bengali, English, Gujarati, Hindi, Kannada, Kashmiri, Konkani, Malayalam, Manipuri, Marathi, Nepali, Oriya, Punjabi, Sanskrit, Sindhi, Tamil, Telugu, and Urdu
Main Religion	Hinduism (83 percent)
Important Holidays	Republic Day, January 26
	Independence Day, August 15
Currency	Indian rupee (Rs. 41 = U.S. $1 as of June 1998)

Opposite: **The Dudhsagar waterfalls in Goa are the highest in India.**

Glossary

Indian Vocabulary

bindi (BIN-dee): a colored dot worn by Indian women on their foreheads. Widows do not wear the bindi.

burfee (BUHR-fee): a sweet food made of milk, nuts, dried fruit, and flavorings.

chaat (CHAHT): a popular spicy Indian snack, sometimes made with fruit.

chapati (cha-PAH-ti): round, flat Indian bread that looks somewhat like a tortilla.

Harijans (HUH-ri-jahn): the name Gandhi gave to the untouchables. It means "children of God."

kabaddi (kuh-BAD-di): an Indian game that combines elements of rugby and wrestling.

langar (LAN-gar): a free meal introduced by Sikh Guru Angad so everyone could sit and eat together.

paan (PAHN): betel nuts and other spices, wrapped in a betel leaf smeared with a lime paste mixture, eaten after a meal.

panchayat raj (puhn-CHA-yat RAHJ): government by a council of elders in Indian villages.

pookkalam (POO-kuh-lum): floral decorations put on Malayalee Hindu homes during Onam in Kerala.

Puranas (puh-RA-nahs): collections of short, simple stories about Hinduism of hymns and chants.

rangoli (rung-GOH-lee): decorative designs, made of plain or colored rice flour mixed in water, drawn on the floors and walls of houses for the Festival of Lights.

salwar-kameez (suhl-WAHR-kuh-MEEZ): the loose pants and tunic often worn by Indian women.

tanpura (TAHN-poo-rah): a four-stringed musical instrument.

Vedas (VEY-dahs): ancient texts of hymns and chants used in Hindu rituals. They include the *Sama Veda, Atharva Veda, Yajur Veda, Brahmanas,* and *Upanishads.*

English Vocabulary

alluvial soil: deposits of sand and mud left behind on flooded land or where a river once flowed.

Aryans: Indo-Europeans from central Asia and Europe.

ascetic: a person who follows a strict way of life for religious reasons.

barren: a dry landscape that has few plants and no trees.

Buddha: the founder of Buddhism.

caste: a social class in India, originally based on occupation. The four castes are Brahmins (priests and scholars), Kshatriyas (warriors and rulers), Vaishyas (merchants and farmers), and Sudras (laborers, servants, and slaves).

deforestation: the cutting down or destruction of all the trees in an area.

Diwali: a festival (the Festival of Lights) celebrated in October or November by Hindus and Jains.

Dravidians: the earliest inhabitants of India.

fresco: a picture painted on a wet plastered wall.

Ganesha: the Hindu god with an elephant's head and human body, the son of gods Shiva and Parvati.

gurdwara: a Sikh temple.

Guru Nanak: the founder of Sikhism.

Hanuman: a monkey god.

henna: a reddish-brown dye made from the leaves of henna plants, used to color hands or hair.

heterogeneous: mixed, diverse.

Hindu Trinity: the three forms of the one great god, Ishwara, consisting of Brahma (the creator), Vishnu (the preserver), and Shiva (the destroyer).

Holi: a major spring festival in February or March, for which Indian people clean their homes and burn old things in bonfires to usher in the new. On the day of the festival, people throw colored water and powder at each other.

Indus Valley Civilization: one of the earliest and most extensive civilizations of the world.

Krishna: a Hindu god who is the incarnation of Vishnu, the god of preservation.

Lok Sabha: the lower house of parliament.

maharaja: the title given to a Hindu prince who rules parts of India, especially major states.

Mahavira: the founder of Jainism, a religion that believes in nonviolence to all living creatures.

mausoleum: a large tomb above ground that contains one or more graves.

minaret: a tall, thin tower attached to a mosque.

Mughals: Muslim rulers of India from the sixteenth to eighteenth centuries.

nirvana: the ultimate state of spiritual enlightenment in Hinduism and Buddhism.

Onam: an important festival in Kerala to mark the end of the monsoon season.

overpopulation: more people living in an area than can be adequately supported by the area's resources.

partition: to divide a country into different parts.

pillage: to steal valuables from a place using violent methods.

poaching: catching or killing animals illegally.

Punjabi: the language spoken by people who live in or come from the Punjab.

Raj: rule, specifically British rule in India.

Rajya Sabha: the upper house of parliament.

sari: a wraparound garment worn by Indian women.

shantytown: a collection of rough huts that houses poor people, usually in or near a large city.

stupa: a dome-shaped monument to Buddha.

subcontinent: a land area smaller than a continent that is made up of a number of countries. The term usually refers to the area that contains India, Pakistan, and Bangladesh.

Taj Mahal: a palace-like mausoleum made of pure white marble built by Shah Jahan in the seventeenth century in memory of his dead wife, Mumtaz Mahal.

tyranny: cruel and oppressive leadership, in which one person has complete control over everyone else.

More Books to Read

Amritsar. Beryl Dhanjal (Macmillan Publishing)

Country Topics for Craft Projects: India. Anita Ganeri and Rachel Wright (Watts Books)

Gandhi: Great Soul. John Severance (Clarion Books)

Hindu. Anita Ganeri (Childrens Press)

India. Sylvia McNair (Childrens Press)

India: The Culture. The Lands, Peoples and Cultures series. Bobbie Kalman (Crabtree Publishing)

India. Festivals of the World series. Falaq Kagda (Gareth Stevens)

India: The People. The Lands, Peoples and Cultures series. Bobbie Kalman (Crabtree Publishing)

The Mughal Empire. Isabel Cervera (Childrens Press)

Videos

Elephant: Lord of the Jungle. (Time-Life Video)

India, the Far South. (World Travel Marketing, Ltd.)

India: Land of Spirit and Mystique. (International Video Network)

North India: Varanasi to the Himalayas. (International Video Network)

Raga: Ravi Shankar. (Apple Films)

Web Sites

www.welcometoIndia.com/culture/

www.historyofIndia.com/home.html

www.devi.net/sari.html

www2.whirlpool.com/html/homelife/cookin/India.htm

Due to the dynamic nature of the Internet, some web sites stay current longer than others. To find additional web sites, use reliable search engines with one or more of the following keywords to help you locate information on India. Keywords: *Diwali, Himalayas, Indian music, Indian mutiny, Indian tigers, Jawaharlal Nehru, Satyajit Ray.*

Index